FREUD *or* REICH ?
Psychoanalysis and Illusion

FREUD
or REICH?

Psychoanalysis
and Illusion

by JANINE CHASSEGUET-SMIRGEL
and BÉLA GRUNBERGER

Translated by
Claire Pajaczkowska

'. . . *an association in which the free development of each
is the condition of the free development of all*'

Free Association Books / London / 1986

English language edition
first published 1986 by
Free Association Books
26 Freegrove Road
London N7 9RQ

Originally published 1976 as
Freud ou Reich? Psychanalyse et Illusion
by Collection Les Abysses, Tchou, Paris

British Library Cataloguing in Publication Data
Chasseguet-Smirgel, Janine
   Freud or Reich? Psychoanalysis & illusion.
   1. Reich, Wilhelm
   I. Title   II. Grunberger, Béla   III. Freud ou
   Reich? : Psychoanalysis + illusion. *English*
   150.19'52'0924   RC339.52.R44

ISBN 0-946960-31-3
ISBN 0-946960-32-1 Pbk

Typeset by Computerised Typesetting Services Limited, London
Printed by Billing & Sons Ltd, Worcester

CONTENTS

But forgive me for drifting into psychoanalysis; I simply can't do anything else. I know, however, that psychoanalysis is not the means of making oneself popular.

Letter from Freud to
Arthur Schnitzler 14 May 1922
(Jones, 444).

You are right: one is in danger of overestimating the frequency of an irreligious attitude among intellectuals.

Letter from Freud to
Marie Bonaparte 19 March 1928
(Jones, 447).

PREFACE TO THE
ENGLISH LANGUAGE EDITION

BORN OF THE student revolution of May '68,
W.R.'s glory enjoyed a spectacular revival. All, or
virtually all his works were translated or reprinted,
not only by the publishers La Pensée Molle (Soft Thinking), not only in pirate editions, but also by a highly
reputable publishing house, known for its high standard
scientific series, which published, among others of Reich's
works, that crazy book *God, Ether and the Devil*. An academic wrote a thick tome entitled *Cent Fleurs pour Wilhelm
Reich* (*One Hundred Flowers for Wilhelm Reich*). This was
right in the middle of the Maoist – or even 'Mao-Spontex'
– period (a movement which claimed to be Maoist and
spontaneous; 'Spontex', incidentally, is the brand name of
washing-up sponges). A Yugoslav film called *W.R.,
Mysteries of the Organism* ('Organism' turned out to be a
misprint by an absent-minded typist or a prudish pro-
ducer; it ought to have read 'orgasm' of course) included a
picture of Wilhelm Reich with a picture of the Pope and
one of Freud on either side of him: no doubt like Christ
between the two robbers, but also the 'revolutionary'

flanked by members of the establishment. There is still no psychoanalytic movement in Yugoslavia to date. In the film, both the leader of the Catholic church and Freud were the targets for arrows being shot, in a majestic and revolutionary gesture, by an anonymous archer.

Like everybody else we had read *Character Analysis*, and like everybody else, we found things of value in it. We had also read *The Function of the Orgasm* and Vol. II, *The Discovery of the Orgone* which we ranked, no doubt in our simple-mindedness, amongst those sad books that bear witness to the tragedy that may befall a human soul. This made us all the more curious to understand the meaning of this sudden revival and adulation of poor W.R.; all the more given that we had hitherto felt for him the kind of sympathy that a tragic fate can elicit.

We began by reading everything that was then being published, at a fiendish pace – at such a pace that one might have been forgiven for believing that the presses were turning night and day at the time, fuelled by some (blue) orgonotic energy, driven by the spirit of W.R. Before long it was not so much the content of the books that interested us but rather the reasons for their revival, all the more since, on closer acquaintance, they tended to be rather reactionary – in every sense of the word. His books stood against lay analysis, homosexuals, against the existence of the infantile within each of us. They stood for a mechanical sexuality, lacking the idealization of the partner, fantasy, in short – love. And above all they stood, as we have tried to show in our book, against the truly revolutionary Freudian discovery, that of infantile sexuality.

In the midst of this, in 1972, *Anti-Oedipus* was pub-

10

lished. Remember? A book which has almost been forgotton now in France. But at the time . . . When we read it we found a revamped Reich, made to seem more sophisticated by being filtered through philosophy and through Lacan. We were talking to a friend, a publisher's commissioning editor, about the outbreak of Reichianism, and its latest, Anti-Oedipal phase. He suggested that we got our ideas down on to paper. That is how this book was started. We think of it as a contribution to the analysis of dissidence within the Freudian psychoanalytic movement. Because of this we feel it will still be relevant for a long time to come.

As we read Claire Pajaczkowska's excellent translation *11* today, we are astounded: can France really have been like that ten years ago? Everything was political then. Nothing is political today, or hardly anything. Who reads Reich these days? Who reads *Anti-Oedipus*? Who is Freudo-Marxist? or even Marxist? A few Communists perhaps, and a few priests. Strange country where, at last, the intellectuals are playing the part which should always have been theirs, the dispassionate and clear-sighted critics of culture and society.

But what will fill the gap left by these ideologies?

Thomas Mann thought that the *Anschluss*, the annexation of Austria into the German Reich, was intended to silence Freud, the 'great destroyer of illusions' as he called him. We have not seen the last of the ideologists yet. Which is why we can but believe in the 'éternel retour', the perennial return, of Wilhelm Reich.

B. Grunberger, J. Chasseguet-Smirgel
Summer 1985

PREFACE

There are times when one has to
resign oneself to being unpopular
in order to be right in the long term.

E. Renan, *Discours et Conférences,*
Oeuvres Complètes, Vol. 1, p. 906.

WILHELM REICH's popularity is probably on
the wane, though, as we shall show, the authors
of *Anti-Oedipus* (Deleuze & Guattari, 1972) are
the unfortunate man's direct descendants, and it does
seem reasonable to predict that he and his followers will
keep coming back into fashion.

It is true to say that Freudian psychoanalysis promises
only relative freedom, whereas Deleuze & Guattari, in
Anti-Oedipus, hold out the promise of 'unlimited possibilities'. Moreover, human beings have an insatiable
longing to regain the perfection experienced at the outset
of life, before the differentiation between subject and outside world. In the Freudian system, the belief that a return
to this primary plenitude is possible would be categorized
as 'Illusion'. Freud discusses illusion in his writings on
religion. In *The Future of an Illusion* (1927, *S.E.*, *21*, 31), it is
defined as 'a belief motivated by a wish-fulfilment which
sets no store by verification from reality'. This definition
obviously extends the concept beyond the province of
religions.

It is a paradox of Freudian psychoanalysis that, whilst consistently struggling against Illusion, it somehow activates it. What we mean is that the unconscious fascinates especially those people who have the strongest yearning for their primary plenitude. They want to use its power for their own ends, to merge into its omnipotence, and so the science which discovered it is treated as if it held the promise of bringing about such a fusion. In fact, if you look at it more closely, when psychoanalysis is practised or undertaken, it does nothing of the sort. It cannot return us to the omnipotence which we experienced as a foetus, or *infans*, when we felt that we were the centre of the world. Psychoanalysis can allow us greater access to potential capacities, but only within the relatively limited constraints of the human condition.

14

Because of this, psychoanalysts and followers of Freud may be tempted either to break with Freud and invest their hope for unity in a form of mysticism or a Utopian ideology, or else to inflect Freudian theory, sometimes unwittingly (as did Reich at first), so as to reconcile it with their longing to recover primary narcissism. It seems that psychoanalysis is particularly vulnerable to this process of being turned into an ideology, if we think of ideology as a belief in the Illusion of the possibility of returning to the lost unity, a unity lost ever since the moment of primary separation.

Political ideologies, however, have to be differentiated from other systems of ideological thought because it is their explicit aim to take power and put their principles into practice. Yet this may be true of all ideologies, since spiritual power tends to become confused with temporal power whenever ideology holds out the promise of total satisfaction. So all ideology is political in this sense, or at least is latently so. Political, economic and social circumstances only activate the human yearning for unity, which lurks in the unconscious, waiting for the propitious moment at which to come forward.

This wish was discovered by Freud in 1914 when he wrote 'Man has . . . shown himself incapable of giving up a satisfaction he had once enjoyed' (*S.E.*, *14*, 94). Here he is referring to the satisfaction of primary narcissism. 'He seeks to recover it in the new form of an ego ideal. What he projects before him as his ideal is the substitute for the lost narcissism of his childhood in which he was his own ideal' (p. 94). Freud also says that: 'The development of the ego consists in a departure from primary narcissism and gives rise to a vigorous attempt to recover that state. This departure is brought about by means of the displacement of libido on to an ego ideal.' He adds that: 'The satisfaction is brought about from fulfilling this ideal' (100), so we can assume that man will forever be searching to make good the lack in various ways, and to fill the gap that exists between the ego and its ideal, in an attempt to return to the contentment that has been torn away from him (J. Chasseguet-Smirgel, 1973). The ego ideal has a central place in Freud's analysis of group phenomena.

15

We feel able to offer the following definition of ideology (a definition to which we will return at the end of the book): it is a system of thought which claims to be total, it is a historical and political interpretation whose (unconscious) aim is the actualization of an illusion, of illusion *par excellence*, that the ego and its ideal can be reunited by a short-cut, via the pleasure principle. The pleasure principle entails the immediate and complete discharge of the drives without any of the deferments and detours that characterize the path of its opposite, the reality principle.

Engels' well-known definition of ideology fits with our definition: 'Ideology is a process accomplished by the so-called thinker consciously, it is true, but with a false consciousness. The real motive forces impelling him remain unknown to him; otherwise it simply would not be an ideological process. Hence he imagines false or seeming motive forces' (F. Engels, 1893, 446). For us, however, the 'real motive forces' comprise the human wish to return to a lost unity (Marx's 'total man', if you like), rather than 'the material life conditions of the persons inside whose heads this process goes on' (F. Engels, 1888, 278). The outcome of this process must give cause for concern to even the most ardent follower of even the noblest and best ideal.

Everything which stands in the way of the realization of the illusion, of which ideology is the by-product, has to be annihilated. The aim of illusion, as we have seen, is the idealization of the ego which is brought about by a fusion of the ego and the ego ideal. However, no idealization can take place without projection, an 'operation whereby qualities, feelings, wishes or even "objects", which the subject refuses to recognize or rejects in himself, are expelled from the self and located in another person or thing' (Laplanche & Pontalis, 349). Various people or concepts can be used as screens for such projections (the Jews, the bourgeoisie, patriarchal or industrial society, for example) and, because they are felt to be an obstacle to the realization of the illusion, have to be ruthlessly annihilated. So murder is committed in the name of the ideal, as were the attacks on the Infidels by the Crusaders on the way to Jerusalem. Every time an illusion is activated a bloodbath follows close behind, however limited the group's resources.

Our definition of ideology obviously includes every system of thought which might hold out the promise of absolute happiness (the Aryans will rule the world for a thousand years, a New Jerusalem will appear before our dazzled eyes, man and civilization will be reconciled, etc.). It excludes all partial economic and political solutions, the whole group of ideas to do with concrete solutions for material problems; in short, all prescriptions which do not claim that 'We'll all get to heaven' (title of a song by Michel Polnareff, 1972).

'An individual's private emotional impulses and intellectual acts', writes Freud in *Group Psychology and the Analysis of the Ego*:

> are too weak to come to anything by themselves and are entirely dependent for this on being reinforced by being repeated in a similar way in the other members of the group. We are reminded of how many of these phenomena of dependence are part of the normal constitution of human society, of how little originality and personal courage are to be found in it, of how much every individual is ruled by those attitudes of the group mind . . . (*S.E. 18*, 117).

In the group situation even reality-testing is entrusted to the ego ideal represented by the group (and sometimes by its leader) which is also responsible for the promotion and protection of illusion. The individual ego gives over its prerogatives to the group. What is true or just is what the

17

group deems to be true or just. He who thinks otherwise is expelled, hounded, killed or labelled insane.

It is actually impossible for a group founded on ideology not to proselytize. It will try to destroy not only its enemies and whatever it sets up as the screen of its projection, but also all those people who remain on the outside, unconvinced. By not participating in the game of the illusion they come to represent the failure of illusion itself. In refusing to hand over reality-testing to the worshippers of the illusion they throw it *ipso facto* into doubt ('if you're not for us you're against us'). It now becomes vital for the group to control the indifferent and the sceptics and to force them to cede the function of reality-testing to the 'believers': 'Der Führer hat immer recht'; 'The Party is always right'.

Obviously it is both dangerous and difficult to be a spoil-sport or kill-joy. (Freud suggests that festivals and manic activity are attempts to unite ego and ideal.) Now, whenever illusion is activated, Freud and Freudian psychoanalysis are characterized as 'spoil-sports'. They represent a flaw in the illusion and, as such, must be attacked, as must also all other manifestations of the *ratio*. In fact, they are attacked, for the reasons we have described, with a violence that is in direct proportion to the extent that they were previously felt to shore up the illusion. Ultimately, they are deemed to be traitors as are the analysts who stay faithful to them.

We would claim that all ideology, as we have defined it, tends to become political in some way and tends to put social reality in its service (even when, and precisely when, it is in contradiction with that reality). Here we find a sort of inevitable movement from theory into practice.

Wilhelm Reich's work is overtly political, although it was not so at the outset; it is possible to see its inevitable and spontaneous development inherent in its original premises. We will try to show that, from the outset, his writings are positioned within the register of Illusion, and are in complete contradiction with Freudian theory. One of the ideas we are putting forward is that the opposition between Freud and Reich is not a result of politics (of Reich's Freudo-Marxism), but rather the politics are a result of the opposition.

It is strange to think that fervent Reichians are unaware of the fundamental and direct contradictions between the ideas of Freud and Reich, and of the extent to which the latter inflects and inverts psychoanalytic theory. It is as if the spell in which the Reichian illusion holds them deprives them of their critical and discursive faculties. Dare we add that Reich's thought lacks rigour, despite the fact that it appears to be systematic? It is all the more interesting, therefore, to try to understand how and why his work, with a conceptual structure which is so fragile in comparison to Freudian theory, is able to exercise such a strong fascination.

19

CHAPTER I

THE IMPLICATIONS OF A RETURN TO FREUD
The Question of Lay Analysis

AFTER A PERIOD of unprecedented popularity, based on a complete misunderstanding, psychoanalysis is now the object of increasingly hostile criticism. Not so long ago Freudian thought was broadcast in the mass media, taught in universities and published in paperback.[1] But at least this loss of popularity has had the beneficial effect of exposing the misunderstanding which lay at the heart of the sudden and false glorification of Freudian psychoanalysis.

Is it, indeed, possible for the work of a man who describes the massive blow to human narcissism, the discovery of the unconscious, to become the basis of a cult, laurel wreaths, triumphal arches, and all? On the title page of *The Interpretation of Dreams* Freud quotes Virgil: '*Flectere si nequeo Superos, Acheronta movebo*' ('And if Heaven I cannot bend, then Hell shall be unleashed'), suggesting that he is aware of the fact that his work unleashes 'Hell', that the ego is seen to be governed by forces beyond its control. The fact that the ego 'is no longer the master in its own house', accounts for the fact that 'the ego cannot consider psychoanalysis favourably and obstinately refuses to believe in it' (*S.E.*, *17*, 143). This cult, then, can only have been the result of a misapprehension, of an alteration (conscious or unconscious) of the meaning and essence of Freud's work.

In fact, the more systematic of today's critiques of psychoanalysis try to limit it to the clinical treatment of neurosis – if, that is, they concede to it any therapeutic value at all. Psychoanalysts are forbidden to stray from the straight and narrow of clinical practice or to use psychoanalysis outside of the analyst-analysand relation. Any analyst who ventures off the path of 'the cure' is immediately accused of a 'reductionism' with regard to whatever phenomena he or she happens to be studying. But an exception is often made for 'Freudo-Marxists' who are, on the contrary, highly acclaimed in so far as, like Reich, they take 'Marxism as a father and psychoanalysis as a mother' and when their work is 'placed explicitly in the service of socialist liberation' (Reich, 1935). It is true that orthodox Marxists are usually unenthusiastic about this type of work, and we will come back to the reasons for this.

But before examining Freudo-Marxism we need to confront the more general question of the status of psychoanalysis *vis-à-vis* socio-cultural phenomena. This means looking at all the implications of the 'return to Freud' which, despite being widely proclaimed, is usually taken up only when it does not conflict with the *Zeitgeist*, but rather panders to it or reinforces it. 'Returning to Freud' means, first of all, trying to find out what he considered to be the essence of psychoanalysis. There is no shortage of texts which can tell us this, starting with those that inform us as to the origins of its discoveries. Freud states this clearly in the 'Postscript' to *The Question of Lay Analysis*:

> I have no knowledge of having had any craving in my early childhood to help suffering humanity . . . In my youth I felt an overpowering need to understand something of the riddles of the world in which we live and perhaps even to contribute something to their solution (*S.E.*, *20*, 253).

Here it is clear that, for Freud, the study of mental illnesses is only one way of reaching a better understanding of the 'riddles of the world'. His committed fight on behalf of lay, or non-medical, analysts is closely correlated to the   23 aims he ascribes to psychoanalysis. In this first of his writings on the question he proceeds, dialectically, to reply to the arguments put forward by an 'impartial person'. (It was, in fact, a matter of convincing a magistrate such as the Public Prosecutor, who stopped the trial of Theodor Reik, who had been charged with illegally practising medicine.) This book, *The Question of Lay Analysis*, contains one of the clearest and most succinct accounts of Freudian theory, and in our search for the essence of his view of psychoanalysis we will cite the one passage which sums up his overall argument:

> We do not consider it at all desirable for psychoanalysis to be swallowed up by medicine and to find its last resting place in a textbook of psychiatry under the heading 'Methods of Treatment', alongside such procedures as hypnotic suggestion, autosuggestion, and persuasion, which, born from our ignorance, have to thank the laziness and cowardice of mankind for their

short-lived effects. It deserves a better fate and, it may
be hoped, will meet with one. As a 'depth psychology', a
theory of the mental unconscious, it can become indispensable to all the sciences which are concerned with
the evolution of human civilization and its major
institutions such as art, religion and the social order. It
has already, in my opinion, afforded these sciences
considerable help in solving their problems. But these
are only small contributions compared with what
might be achieved if historians of civilization, psychologists of religion, philologists and so on would agree
themselves to handle the new instrument of research
24   which is at their service. [In this context Freud is
referring to specialists in the 'human' or 'social' sciences, having completed their psychoanalytic training
and treating patients.] The use of analysis for the treatment of the neuroses is only one of its applications; the
future will perhaps show that it is not the most important one. In any case it would be wrong to sacrifice all
the other applications to this single one, just because it
touches on the circle of medical interest (248).

The following footnote, from the book *Wilhelm Reich* by
J.M. Palmier, is incomprehensible to us:

In 1926 a patient brought charges against his analyst,
(Theodor Reik), a lay analyst, for the illegal practice of
medicine. Reik won the trial but Freud seized this
opportunity to limit the practice of analysis by non-
doctors and to fix the status of the analyst through the
Associations, which alone could confer the qualifica-
tion. This essay, unfortunately little known, deserves to
be studied carefully (Palmier, 1969, 23–4).

However, there is nothing in the text or context, nor in
Freud's subsequent views, that might suggest we should
take *The Question of Lay Analysis* for anything other than
what it is, a passionate plea for lay analysis and for
preserving the spirit of psychoanalysis. Palmier's position, supporting Reich, pushes him towards a certain
Manichaeism, avoiding the facts of the case. On the one
hand, we are given Freud, the conservative, to whom
Palmier ascribes a background in 'the Old Viennese bourgeoisie' (150), whereas he actually came from a working,
Jewish Moravian family (originally from the Rhine near
Cologne). On the other hand, we have Reich the revolutionary. Having constructed such a scenario the former   25
could only be seen to bear allegiance to the medical élite.
In actual fact, it was Reich who fought actively for the
practice of psychoanalysis to be limited to medical doctors, as he clearly stated:

> He [Freud] made great mistakes there. I think it was a
> very great mistake in his fight against the chauvinism in
> medicine when he protected Reik. Theodor Reik was in
> trouble once in Vienna. He was attacked by someone
> for practising medicine. Freud supported him. And
> from that 'lay analysis' developed. Freud gave very
> strong support to the lay analyst. I don't know how you
> feel about it but I tell you quite frankly I think Freud
> made a very grave mistake. The admission of lay ana-
> lysts into natural scientific psychoanalysis was a very
> great mistake (Reich, 1952, 253).

Even before the debate on lay analysis, as early as 1925
Freud wrote *An Autobiographical Study* (*S.E.*, *20*) in which
he listed the extra-therapeutic applications of psycho-

analysis and said 'they are essential to a correct apprecia-
tion of the nature and value of psychoanalysis' (70). After
outlining the themes of his own contributions to the field,
he concludes that 'it is no longer possible to restrict the
practice of psychoanalysis to doctors and to exclude laymen from it' (70).

In the 1927 'Postscript' cited above Freud reaffirms his
views. He addressed his article not only to the 'impartial
person' but also to his colleagues, many of whom were
antagonistic to lay analysis. In this article he proposes
that a psychoanalytic education should include 'elements
of the sciences of mind, psychology, the history of civilization, and sociology as well as anatomy, biology and the
study of evolution'. He considered this 'an ideal, no
doubt, but an ideal which can and must be realized'.
More generally, Freud describes himself as 'a defender of
the intrinsic worth of psychoanalysis and of its indepen-
dence from its medical applications', and would like 'to be
sure that the therapy will not destroy the science'. It
seems clear in this case that the therapy is only one of the
possible applications of psychoanalysis, one which must
not supplant all the others but which, whilst helping
patients, is aimed at making further contributions to
psychoanalytic science in general.

26

> For practical reasons we have been in the habit – and
> this is true of my own publications – of distinguishing
> between medical psychoanalysis and applied psycho-
> analysis. But this is not a logical distinction. The true
> line of division is between *scientific* analysis and its
> *applications* alike, in medical and in non-medical fields
> (257).

At around the same time (1925–6) the *Encyclopaedia Britannica* asked Freud to contribute an article, 'Psychoanalysis'. In this article he writes, 'The future will probably give greater significance to psychoanalysis as the science of the unconscious than to the therapeutic process'. Again he mentions the extra-therapeutic applications 'such as social anthropology, the study of religion, literary history, and education' (*S.E.*, *20*, 268).

For Freud the problem of lay analysis was very closely linked with his aim of keeping psychoanalysis a scientific body of work with a scope much wider than its medical applications. This became a great source of conflict within the psychoanalytic movement, especially because of the attitudes of those Americans hostile to 'laymen', who were joined by analysts from elsewhere. In 1928 Freud wrote to Ferenczi: 27

> The internal development of psychoanalysis is everywhere proceeding contrary to my intentions away from lay analysis and becoming a pure medical speciality, and I regard this as fateful for the future of analysis (Jones, 297).

In 1929 Freud wrote to Eitingon that he envisaged 'a friendly separation with the Americans. I have no desire to give way in the lay question, and there is no way of bridging the gulf'. Ever since 1925 in his *Autobiographical Study* Freud had accused the American Association of 'mixing much water with its wine' and by 1929 he was pushing much harder for a split. Freud declared that opposition to lay analysis was 'the last mask of the resistance against psychoanalysis, and the most dangerous of all' (Jones, 298). Political events and the emigration of

European analysts to America made the issue a comparatively dormant one. The war and then Freud's death seemed to conclude the dispute, with the Americans refusing non-medical affiliation to the International Psychoanalytic Association and to their regional associations. However, on 5 July 1938 Freud had written to an American analyst:

> Dear Mr Schnier,
> I cannot imagine how that silly rumour of my having changed my views about the problem of Lay-Analysis may have originated. The fact is, I have never repudiated these views and I insist on them even more intensely than before, in the face of the obvious American tendency to turn psychoanalysis into a mere housemaid of psychiatry.
> Sincerely yours,
> Sigm. Freud   (Jones, 300–1).

It is up to the reader whether to connect this fact with the relative erosion of a part of American psychoanalysis.[2] In any case, the connection has been made by one American analyst, Kurt Eissler (1965). It must be noted, on the other hand, that to be true to Freud it is not enough simply to accept non-doctors among the membership of psychoanalytic societies, if this is only to confine them to practising therapy, whilst condemning and criticizing attempts to apply his theories outside the field of clinical practice.

Although Freud was right to link lay analysis and the application of psychoanalysis to solutions for the 'riddles of the world' it seems that this anthropological project elicits the strongest resistances. These resistances go well beyond simply defending the interests of a group; they are

28

only the surface manifestation covering very deep defences against the nature of psychoanalysis as Freud conceived of it.

CHAPTER II

THE IMPLICATIONS OF A RETURN TO FREUD
The Search for Universals

PSYCHOANALYSIS IS not an addition to the psychiatric arsenal of treatments, alongside Largactyl and electric shock. It claims to be not only a key to understanding humanity, but *the* key which unlocks the doors to knowledge of the species, in all aspects of our behaviour and activities. It should be remembered that this was the view of the founder of psychoanalysis, however much one may disagree.

We should also remember that Freud thought that the individual and groups were similarly structured:

A similar application of its points of view, its hypotheses and its findings has enabled psychoanalysis to throw light on the origins of our great cultural institutions – on religion, morality, justice and philosophy. By examining the primitive psychological situations which were able to provide the motive for creations of this kind, it has been in a position to reject certain attempts at an explanation that were based on too superficial a psychology and to replace them with a more penetrating insight.

Psychoanalysis has established an intimate connection between these psychical achievements of individuals on the one hand and societies on the other by *postulating one and the same dynamic source for both of them* [our italics]. Our knowledge of the neurotic illnesses of individuals has been of much assistance to our understanding of the great social institutions. For the neuroses themselves have turned out to be attempts to find individual solutions for the problems of compensating for unsatisfied wishes, while the institutions seek to provide social solutions for these same problems. ('The Claims of Psychoanalysis to Scientific Interest'; 1913, *S.E.*, *13*, 185–6).

31

In the same year, writing *Totem and Taboo*, Freud reaffirms that:

This single comparison between taboo and obsessional neurosis is enough to enable us to gather the nature of the relation between the different forms of neurosis and cultural institutions, and to see how it is that the study of the psychology of the neuroses is important for an understanding of the growth of civilization (*S.E.*, *13*, 73).

In this same work which, as he wrote to Abraham, he considered as striking an unequivocal blow against religion, he again raises the question of the similarity of structure between the individual and the collective psyche:

Neuroses exhibit on the one hand striking and far-reaching points of agreement with those great social institutions, art, religion and philosophy. But on the other hand they seem like distortions of them. It might be maintained that a case of hysteria is a caricature of a work of art, that an obsessional neurosis is a caricature of a religion, and that a paranoic delusion is a caricature of a philosophical system (73).

In his essay on 'Obsessive Actions and Religious Practices' (1907), Freud's first study of religion, he points out that the surface similarity between an obsessive 'ceremonial' and a religious ritual corresponds, in fact, to deeper structures. At the deeper level we can understand the meaning of the religious ritual because of the aetiological study of neurotic ceremonials. The analogy is not merely formal; it is a result of the equivalence that exists, as Freud tries to show, between obsessional symptoms and religious practices. This equivalence is due to their identical functions. In both cases we find some degree of protection from a previously repressed re-emerging sexual drive, which produces intense guilt feelings. They also have in common the mechanism of displacement. It is in this essay that we find the famous statement that obsessional neurosis is a private religion and that religion is a universal obsessional neurosis:

> One might venture to regard obsessional neurosis as a pathological counterpart of the formation of a religion, and to describe that neurosis as an individual religiosity and religion as a universal obsessional neurosis (1907, *S.E.*, *9*, 126).

Freud returns to the deep structures underlying both

obsessional neurosis and religion in *The Future of an Illusion*
(1927, *S.E.*, *21*, 1–56) and in *Moses and Monotheism* (1939,
S.E., *23*, 1–137).

In 1921, in *Group Psychology and the Analysis of the Ego*
(*S.E.*, *18*, 65–143), one of Freud's basic premises is that:
'the opposition between individual psychology and social
psychology . . . loses much of its sense when one examines
it more closely'. In this study of groups such as the crowd,
the church and the army, Freud constantly refers to processes on the level of the individual ego in order to understand group processes. He compares the group to the
individual prototype in a sort of dialectical way which
supports his thesis on the homogeneity between the indi-   *33*
vidual and the group, for example he discusses the idealization of leaders by their groups and compares this
process to the state of being in love and the action of
hypnosis. This leads him to conclude that group
behaviour does not depend on any extraneous psychic
formations in the individual. The phenomena that occur
in groups are not a creation, but the group simply acts on
tendencies that are latent in the individual.

> The individual in the crowd finds himself in conditions
> which permit him to release repression of his uncon-
> scious tendencies. The apparently new characteristics
> which he manifests there are precisely only manifesta-
> tions of that unconscious where the seed of all that is
> bad in the human soul is catalogued.

In the 'Postscript' to *An Autobiographical Study* (1935)
Freud again writes:

> My interest, after making a lifelong detour through

the natural sciences, medicine and psychotherapy, returned to the cultural problems which fascinated me long before, when I was a youth scarcely old enough for thinking. At the very climax of my psychoanalytic work in 1912, I had already attempted in *Totem and Taboo* to make use of the newly discovered findings of analysis in order to investigate the origins of religion and morality. I now carried this work a stage further in two later essays, *The Future of an Illusion* (1927) and *Civilization and its Discontents* (1930). I perceived ever more clearly that the events of human history, the interactions between human nature, cultural development and the precipitates of primaeval experiences (the most prominent example of which is religion) are no more than a reflection of the dynamic conflicts between the ego, the id and the superego, which psychoanalysis studies in the individual – are the very same processes repeated upon a wider stage (*S.E.*, *20*, 72).

34

Given these examples we can now see a decompartmentalization between different types of phenomena (especially between neuroses and institutions, between the individual and the group) which can be seen as having a fundamental equivalence. We would like to show, briefly, that this inter-relationship, which confirms the equivalence between various human activities, is not something fortuitous, but that it is integral to the essence of the psychoanalytic process.

We should remember that psychoanalysis as a method of treatment was developed, for the most part, through material from 'normal subjects'. Freud considered the theory of dreams to be the 'cornerstone' of psychoanalysis, and dreaming is a universal phenomenon, common to all humans. It was the theory of dreams that facilitated the discovery of the laws of the unconscious, the primary process, and a model of the psychic apparatus; and dreaming was taken to be the 'normal' prototype of pathological phenomena (1900, *S.E.*, *4–5*). Further illustrations of mental functioning were provided in *The Psychopathology of Everyday Life* (1901, *S.E.*, *6*) which deals with slips of the tongue and mistakes in everyday life, also by jokes in *Jokes and Their Relation to the Unconscious* (1905, *S.E.*, *8*), and in the study of literature undertaken in *Delusions and Dreams in Jensen's 'Gradiva'* (1907, *S.E.*, *9*), to cite only a few of the works from the turn of the century –   *35* that is, from the dawn of Freudianism. At the same time Freud shows, particularly in *The Interpretation of Dreams* and in *Three Essays on the Theory of Sexuality*, the existence of infantile sexuality, the Oedipus complex, and the primary drives, this time at the level of the contents of the unconscious. The Oedipus complex is universally present in the unconscious and the primary drives are identical in all humans. Thus the transition from the sphere of mental disorders to that of the 'normal' psyche is made possible. The difference between the normal and the pathological, like the difference between the individual and the group, disappears at a certain point, giving rise to the idea of a human psyche governed by laws common to all humanity and structured as an intangible kernel. This is clearly demonstrated in this passage from 'Thoughts for the Times on War and Death':

> In reality, there is no such thing as 'eradicating' evil.
> Psychological – or, more strictly speaking, psychoana-

lytic – investigation shows instead that the deepest
essence of human nature consists of *instinctual impulses
which are of an elementary nature, which are similar in all men*
and which aim at the satisfaction of certain primal
needs (1915, *S.E.*, *14*, 281; our italics).

Bearing in mind that Freud defines the drive as a 'frontier
concept between the mental and the physical' (*Three
Essays*; 1905, *S.E.*, *7*, 168), these 'instinctual impulses of an
elementary nature, similar in all men' can only be the
primary drives, whose biological roots account for their
uniformity. The source of a drive is always physical, an
excitation occurring in an organ which gives rise to internal tension requiring discharge.

36

The primary drives exist in all humans and their biological roots imply a continuity between the human and
animal kingdoms. This continuity between us and the
animal kingdom Freud considered to be the 'second blow
to human narcissism', the 'biological blow to human narcissism' dealt us by Darwin:

> Man is not a being different from animals or superior to
> them; he himself is of animal descent . . . The acquisi-
> tions he has subsequently made have not succeeded in
> effacing the evidences, both in his physical structure
> and in his mental dispositions, of his parity with them
> ('A Difficulty in the Path of Psychoanalysis'; 1917, *S.E.*,
> *17*, 141).

But there is, on the other hand, a characteristic that is
specific to humans which is equally universal according to
Freudian psychoanalysis. This is, as you will have
guessed, the Oedipus complex.

Without reiterating the complete history of the discovery of the Oedipus complex, or the history of Freud's debates on it, or the debates that this concept sparked off (and still does), it may be useful to mention a few theses that summarize his views. The temporal and spatial universality of the Oedipus complex, in other words, its horizontal (geographic) and vertical (historic) universality is confirmed, by Freud, in *The Question of Lay Analysis:*

> Nothing has damaged it [psychoanalysis] more in the good opinion of its contemporaries than its hypothesis of the Oedipus complex as a structure universally bound to human destiny . . . Incestuous wishes are a primordial human heritage and have never been fully overcome . . . It is in complete harmony with these lessons of history and mythology that we find incestuous wishes still present and operative in the childhood of the individual (1926, *S.E.*, *20*, 213–4).

37

Here, with twenty-eight years' hindsight and slightly different words, Freud is restating his first formulation of the Oedipus complex as we find it in the famous letter to Fliess of 15 October 1897, in which he writes of his self-analysis: 'the Greek myth seizes on a compulsion which everyone recognizes because he has felt traces of it in himself' (Freud, 1954, 223). We see that from the outset he implicitly posits the universality of the Oedipus complex, which has been confirmed by ethnologists in the form of the universality of the incest taboo. Also, we should remember that according to Freud, nothing human can be foreign to us, for the very reason that these universals exist, which is what makes psychoanalytic

interpretation possible, amongst other things. Accounting for our capacity to interpret psychic facts (mediated,
of course, by training, and disregarding individual differences) Freud asks: 'Why do you choose to except your
own mental processes from the rule of the law which you
recognize in other people's?' (1926, *S.E.*, *20*, 219).

Moreover, the Oedipus complex can itself be considered to have a biological basis, not only because Freud
saw in Rank's hypothesis of the birth trauma (which he
rejected in its complete form) a glimpse of the 'biological
background of the Oedipus complex' (Jones, 61), but also
because the complex as a human characteristic has to be
38   related to another specifically human characteristic. This
is the small human's long dependence on its parents, as a
consequence of its prematurity. Throughout his writings
Freud insisted on this factor, the '*Hilflosigkeit*' – helplessness or distress. In *Inhibitions, Symptoms and Anxiety* Freud
assigns the role of the 'biological' cause of the neuroses to
this prematurity which produces feelings of primary
helplessness:

> The biological factor is the long period of time during
> which the young of the human species is in a condition
> of helplessness and dependence. Its intra-uterine exist-
> ence seems to be short in comparison with that of most
> animals, and it is sent into the world in a less finished
> state. As a result, the influence of the real external
> world upon it is intensified and an early differentiation
> between the ego and the id is promoted. Moreover, the
> dangers of the external world have a greater import-
> ance for it, so that the value of the object which can
> alone protect it against them and take the place of its

former intra-uterine life is enormously enhanced. The biological factor, then, establishes the earliest situations of danger and creates the need to be loved which will accompany the child through the rest of its life (*S.E.*, *20*,154–5).

In the 'Project for a Scientific Psychology' he discusses the importance of prematurity for the human psychosexual organization:

> At first, the human organism is incapable of bringing about the specific action. It takes place by extraneous help, when the attention of an experienced person is drawn to the child's state by discharge along the path of internal change [e.g. by the child's screaming]. In this way this path of discharge acquires a secondary function of the highest importance, that of *communication*, and the initial helplessness of human beings is the *primal source* of all *moral motives* (*S.E.*, *1*, 318).

39

In his structural theory of the psychic apparatus Freud attributes the moral motives of the 'superego', at least in part, to primary helplessness:

> If we consider once more the origin of the superego as we have described it, we shall recognize that it is the outcome of two highly important biological factors: namely the duration in man of his childhood helplessness and dependence, and the fact of his Oedipus complex (which we have traced back to the interruption of libidinal development by the latency period and so to the diphasic onset of man's sexual life) (1923, *S.E.*, *19*, 35).

Whilst the connection between the Oedipus complex (a human universal) and prematurity (a biological characteristic that is species-specific) is not made explicit in Freud's work, it is not difficult to see an implicit connection frequently made in his work. It is impossible to think of the Oedipus complex except in terms of this attachment to objects which Freud described in the 'Project' and in *Inhibitions, Symptoms and Anxiety*. It is this attachment which contributes to the specificity of human love, and we will return to this point. But contrary to what exists in other animals, this attachment tends to exist all the more strongly where it has no sexual release. This fact is a consequence of the prohibition of incest, a universal prohibition which results in the Oedipus complex proper. In fact, some analysts have recently related this prohibition itself to human species prematurity. It is then understood as the result of the anachronistic relation between oedipal wishes (which, according to Freud, appear between two years and five years of age, whereas in Melanie Klein's opinion they are active from the age of six months) and the physiological capacity to satisfy these wishes. The introduction of a prohibition or interdiction (which is of external origin, coming from the father) diminishes the painful sense of inadequacy, and protects the subject from narcissistic injury (Grunberger, 1956).

'If the three-year-old boy had the strength of a twenty-year-old man', wrote Diderot, 'he would kill his father and sleep with his mother.' But it is precisely the case that the three-year-old boy does have wishes that he is incapable of satisfying. The painful inadequacy of the oedipal child was established by Freud himself – but without his linking this to the universality of the incest taboo. We know that

40

he traced the origins of the incest taboo back to the
murder of the father by the sons of the primal horde,
which he referred to as the 'scientific myth' of the recon-
struction of human prehistory.

> The early efflorescence of infantile sexual life is doomed
> to extinction because its wishes are incompatible with
> reality and the inadequate stage of development which
> the child has reached. That efflorescence comes to an
> end in the most distressing circumstances and to the
> accompaniment of the most painful feelings. Loss of
> love and failure leave behind them a permanent injury
> to self-regard in the form of a narcissistic scar, which in
> my opinion, as well as in Marcinowski's (1918), con-
> tributes more than anything to the 'sense of inferiority'
> which is so common in neurotics. The child's sexual
> researches, on which limits are imposed by his physical
> development, lead to no satisfactory conclusion; hence
> such later complaints as 'I can't accomplish anything; I
> can't succeed in anything'. The tie of affection which
> binds the child as a rule to the parent of the opposite sex
> succumbs to disappointment, to a vain expectation
> of satisfaction or to jealousy over the birth of a new baby
> – unmistakable proof of the infidelity of the object of
> the child's affections. His own attempt to make a
> baby himself, carried out with tragic seriousness, fails
> shamefully. The lessening amount of affection he
> receives, the increasing demands of education, hard
> words and an occasional punishment – these show him
> at last the extent to which he has been scorned (1920,
> S.E., 18, 20–21).

41

This is the drama of the oedipal child as Freud describes it

in *Beyond the Pleasure Principle*. The inadequacy of the child
due to its immaturity is absolutely central to the oedipal
drama. In fact, the prohibition of incest contains – and
probably disguises – the incapacity for incest. In 'The
Dissolution of the Oedipus Complex' (1924) Freud
writes:

> To an ever-increasing extent the Oedipus complex
> reveals its importance as the central phenomenon of
> early childhood. After that, its dissolution takes place;
> it succumbs to repression, as we say, and is followed by
> the latency period. It has not yet become clear, how-
> ever, what it is that brings about its destruction.
> Analyses seem to show it is the experience of painful
> disappointments. The little girl likes to regard herself as
> what her father loves above all else; but the time comes
> when she has to endure a harsh punishment from him
> and she is cast out of her fool's paradise. The boy
> regards his mother as his own property; but he finds one
> day that she has transferred her love and solicitude to a
> new arrival. Reflection must deepen our sense of the
> importance of these influences, for it will emphasize the
> fact that distressing experiences of this sort, which act
> in opposition to the content of the complex, are inevit-
> able. Even when no special events occur, like the ones
> we have mentioned as examples, the absence of the
> satisfaction hoped for, the *continued denial of the desired
> baby*, must in the end lead the small lover to turn away
> from his hopeless longing. In this way the Oedipus
> complex would go to its destruction from its lack of
> success, from the effects of its *internal impossibility* (*S.E.*,
> *19*, 173; our italics). [Freud repeatedly confirms that

42

the oedipal child wishes to make a baby. This accentu-
ates the anachronism we describe between the moment
at which oedipal wishes arise and the physiological
means at the child's disposal.]

The relation between the Oedipus complex and the castration complex can be traced back, too, to the prematurity of human birth. Because of its inadequacy the
child hopes to acquire the genital organs of the parent of
the same sex. The little boy wants to castrate his father
and to take possession of his penis. At the same time,
children of both sexes want to separate the parents by
destroying their genital organs. The castration complex
seems to be, at least in part, the child's fear of retaliation
as a consequence of his own castration wishes towards the
adult.

43

The castration complex too is something common to all
humans. In conjunction with the 'internal impossibility',
the castration complex gives rise to the dissolution of the
Oedipus complex and to the inauguration of the superego.
Summarizing the classical Freudian view, the male child
implicates his penis in his oedipal wishes, although in a
rather vague way as he does not know that the mother
possesses a genital organ which is the counterpart of his
own. The oedipal phase is accompanied by phallic masturbation, the unconscious object of which is the mother.
The father is a rival which the child wishes away in order
to replace him. According to Freud, the castration fears
awakened by masturbatory activity have three causes.
Firstly, there are real threats; secondly, the existence of
previous situations in which parts of himself have already
been taken from the child (the breast, which was at one

time experienced as part of his own body, faeces and, earlier still, the uterine environment at the moment of birth). Finally, the sight of the female genital organs, without a penis, which are interpreted by the male child as a confirmation of the threat, since he sees that there are beings without penises, who are, in other words, castrated. This conjunction of factors gives rise to an anxiety of such an intensity that the child abandons his sensual investment in the mother and internalizes the prohibition of incest. The prohibition is experienced as coming from the father, and the superego is thus inaugurated. The Oedipus complex is dissolved, the child gives up the function of his penis in order to save the organ and enters into the latency period. This, according to Freud, is the process which explains the diphasic organization of human sexuality. By diphasic is meant the fact that there is a period of latency following the dissolution of the Oedipus complex and lasting until puberty.

44

So, Freud posits a number of 'universals' which are transhistorical and are common to all humanity. These are the primary drives, species prematurity and its consequences, the Oedipus complex, the castration complex and the superego (with the prohibition of incest). In our view, on the one hand these 'universals' have their roots in biology and on the other they constitute a kind of template for human nature. There is no doubt that 'Man' exists, for Freud, and in such a way as to be independent of the material conditions in which he is immersed. We are able to understand mankind, through history, across socio-economic regimes, civilizations, races, continents, in health or illness, because men resemble one another, because of certain, fundamentally biological, invariables.

Thus it is that a Greek myth expressed in a tragedy written 430 BC in a slave society can also find expression in an English play from the early seventeenth century written in a feudal society, and can be taken as a model for the human psyche, in late nineteenth-century Vienna, taking two of the examples that Freud chose in discovering the Oedipus complex.

> Every member of the audience was once a budding Oedipus in phantasy, and this dream fulfilment played out in reality causes everyone to recoil in horror, with the full measure of repression which separates his infantile from his present state. The idea has passed through my head that the same thing may lie at the root of Hamlet (Freud, 1954, 224).

45

Neither does Freud hesitate to compare the results of his self-analysis with material from his patients saying: 'I can only analyse myself with objectively acquired knowledge' (Freud, 1954, 234), referring to his daily clinical practice.

Freud often used the term 'human nature'. For example, in 1930 in *Civilization and its Discontents* he wrote:

> The Communists believe that they have found the path to deliverance from our evils. According to them, man is wholly good and is well-disposed to his neighbour; but the institution of private property has corrupted his nature . . . I have no concern with any economic criticisms of the Communist system . . . But I am able to recognize that the psychological premises on which the system is based are an untenable illusion. In abolishing private property . . . we have in no way altered the differences in power and influence which are misused

by aggressiveness, nor have we altered anything in its nature. Aggressiveness was not created by property. It reigned almost without limit in primitive times, when property was still very scanty, and it already shows itself in the nursery almost before property has given up its primal anal form . . . We cannot easily foresee what new paths the development of civilization could take; but one thing we can expect, and that is that this indestructible feature of human nature will follow it there (*S.E.*, *21*, 112–14).

Again on the subject of Communism, Freud says of 'human nature':

46

And although practical Marxism has mercilessly cleared away all idealistic systems and illusions, it has itself developed illusions which are no less questionable and unprovable than the earlier ones . . . But a transformation of human nature such as this is highly improbable . . . In just the same way as religion, Bolshevism too must compensate its believers for the sufferings and deprivations of their present life by promises of a better future in which there will no longer be any unsatisfied need. This paradise, however, is to be in this life, instituted on earth and thrown open within a foreseeable time ('A *Weltanschauung?*';1932, *S.E.*, *22*, 180).

Yet, whilst awaiting the hypothetical transformation of human nature, the Bolsheviks are obliged to punish and to prohibit:

And we should be politely asked to say how things could be managed differently. This would defeat us. I

could think of no advice to give. I should admit that the
conditions of this experiment would have deterred me
and those like me from undertaking it; but we are not
the only people concerned. There are men of action,
unshakable in their convictions, inaccessible to doubt,
without feeling for the suffering of others if they stand in
the way of their intentions. We have to thank men of
this kind for the fact that the tremendous experiment of
producing a new order of this kind is actually being
carried out in Russia . . . Unluckily neither our scepticism nor the fanatical faith of the other side gives a hint
as to how the experiment turns out . . . Even then, to be
sure, we shall still have to struggle for an incalculable   *47*
time with the difficulties which the untameable
character of human nature presents to every kind of
social community (181).

Even when the term 'human nature' is not mentioned
there can be no doubt as to the implicit presence of the
concept in Freud's work, increasingly as it progresses.
Thus, in 'Why War?' (1933, *S.E.*, *22*, 204–13), he writes:

It is a general principle, then, that conflicts of interest
between men are settled by the use of violence. This is
true of the whole animal kingdom, from which men
have no business to exclude themselves . . . In addition
to this, killing an enemy satisfied an instinctual inclination which I will have to mention later . . . There is no
use in trying to get rid of men's aggressive inclinations
. . . The Russian Communists, too, hope to be able to
cause human aggressiveness to disappear by guaran-
teeing the satisfaction of all material needs and by
establishing equality in other respects among all the

members of a community. That, in my opinion, is an illusion . . . In any case, as you yourself have remarked, there is no question of getting rid entirely of human aggressive impulses; it is enough to try to divert them to such an extent that they need not find expression in war. After all, it [war] seems to be quite a natural thing, to have a good biological basis and in practice to be scarcely avoidable.

It is obviously no mere coincidence that it is especially when debating Marxism and its applications that Freud brings up the 'human nature' argument. Today it seems that anyone who might try and use this argument would immediately be labelled 'reactionary' or, even worse, 'idealist'. In fact, the second of these epithets would only apply to a disembodied theory of 'human nature', one severed from its biological roots. Since the concept of 'human nature' contradicts Marxism, and as the biological basis of Freud's theory means that it cannot be classed among the idealist doctrines, we find that many Marxists will choose Lacanianism in preference to classical Freudianism, as Lacan has tended to abandon all references to biology. In fact, the two equally materialist theories of Freud and Marx do present us with troublesome conflict and rivalry.

48

We believe and have tried to show that Freudian theory is not 'disembodied', that it is based in biology. We might also add, axiomatically, that the problem is not so much that of showing an idea to be reactionary or progressive, but of finding out whether it is true or false. In other words, it is important to find out the extent of a theory's scientific validity.

CHAPTER III

THE IMPLICATIONS OF
A RETURN TO FREUD
The Primacy of Internal Factors

BECAUSE OF HIS discovery of human 'universals', and because of his concept of a human nature which includes characteristics that we share with other animals as well as ones that are uniquely human, Freud was led to claim that 'psychoanalysis cannot well be handled like a pair of glasses that one puts on for reading and takes off when one goes for a walk'.

Freud's theory always kept a place for such biological facts as constitution, heredity and phylogenetic memory traces. Here we might mention that, for Freud, 'primal' or originary – '*Urphantasien*' – fantasies (those of intra-uterine life, of the primal scene, of castration and seduction), have an autonomous existence in the individual independent of his real lived personal history. In addition to these primal fantasies there are also the infantile sexual theories which may be produced spontaneously by 'all human children'. Even if one disagrees with the concept of genetically transmitted structures, these fantasies can be understood. It may be that because of the primary drives and the organic erogenous zones of their sources, and also because of the fact that every human being is one of two different sexes, similar templates are produced, through which fantasy life is formed and channelled, giving rise to similar structures regardless of personal history.

Freud wrote:

> I have told you that psychoanalysis began as a method of treatment; but I did not want to commend it to your interest as a method of treatment but on account of the . . . information it gives us about what concerns human beings most of all – their own nature – and on account of the connections it discloses between the most different of their activities ('Explanations, Applications and Orientations'; 1932, *S.E.*, *22*, 156–7).

50

Furthermore, 'Since nothing that men make or do is understandable without the cooperation of psychology, the applications of psychoanalysis to numerous fields of knowledge, in particular to those of the mental sciences, came about of their own accord, pushed their way to the front'. This did not happen easily; 'The more a scientific work has practical applications the more bitterly it is contested' (145).

Yet Freud goes even further; psychoanalysis is not only an indispensable research tool, it comes to occupy the privileged place of being *the* science fundamental to all the human sciences. We frequently find this idea in his work. For instance, in *Totem and Taboo*, towards the end of the book he writes a footnote:

> Since I am used to being misunderstood I think it worth while to insist explicitly that the derivations which I have proposed in these pages do not in the least over-

III]   THE PRIMACY OF INTERNAL FACTORS

look the complexity of the phenomena under review. All that they claim is to have added a new factor to the sources, known or still unknown, of religion, morality and society – a factor based on a consideration of the implications of psychoanalysis. I must leave to others the task of synthesizing the explanation into a unity. It does, however, follow from the nature of the new contribution that it could not play any other than a central part in such a synthesis, even though powerful emotional resistances might have to be overcome before its great importance was recognized (1912–13, *S.E.*, *13*, 157).

This footnote, which starts out somewhat tentatively, concludes with an assertion about the role of psychoanalysis in the interpretation of human culture, the imperialist tone of which no one can fail to notice. It refers to the end of *Totem and Taboo* where Freud shows that religion, morality, society and art all have their origins in the Oedipus complex:

> It seems to me a most surprising discovery that the problems of social psychology, too, should prove soluble on the basis of one single concrete point – man's relation to his father (1912–13, *S.E.*, *13*, 157).

Once again there can be no question that this is more than a passing opinion on the role of psychoanalysis in the social sciences. In 'A *Weltanschauung*?' he states: 'For sociology too, dealing as it does with the behaviour of people in society, cannot be anything but applied psychology. Strictly speaking there are only two sciences: psychology, pure and applied, and natural science' (1932,

S.E., *22*, 179). It may be useful to clarify a misunderstanding which is often made of this *New Introductory Lecture*. Freud refused to consider psychoanalysis as a *Weltanschauung*, a world-view, because he considered it a science. Thus, 'it asserts that there are no sources of knowledge of the universe other than the intellectual working-over of . . . what we call research, and [not from] revelation, intuition or divination' (159). Here Freud contrasts psychoanalysis as a form of scientific knowledge to philosophy, in so far as the latter uses extra-scientific methods, and especially to religion. Moreover, religious and philosophical systems claim to explain the world according to a single principle. This is not true of psychoanalysis, which progresses, within its field, by using forms of knowledge which are scientific. It is at this point, we feel, that the misunderstanding takes place. The absence of a *Weltanschauung* proper to psychoanalysis does not mean – as this *New Introductory Lecture* demonstrates – that it must only be applied as a method to a limited area of study, nor that it must remain silent on the broader issues of culture. On the contrary, the fact that Freud categorized it as a science provides it with immense scope: everything that is not included in the natural sciences.

Furthermore, as with a number of Freud's works, it is useful to understand this lecture within the context of the debates in psychoanalytic circles of the time, particularly in relation to dissident theories, to which Freud's writings are often implicit replies. In this case, we should bear in mind the report that Reich read to Freud in 1930 entitled 'Psychoanalysis and *Weltanschauung*', in which he attacked analytic neutrality and claimed that psychoanalysis gives rise to a world-view leading to the overthrow of existing

social institutions. According to Reich, analysts must necessarily be politically committed to revolutionary Marxism. In the *New Introductory Lecture* quoted Freud opposes
this, presenting an account of Marxism which criticizes
those of its assumptions that seemed wrong to him. These
assumptions he thought mistaken, illusory, and as collud-
ing in a religious kind of thinking. In wanting to classify
psychoanalysis as a branch of science he ascribes to it an
objectivity which is the opposite of political commitment.
Freud was concerned with social institutions to the extent
that they form part of a subject of study. We saw that
Freud places psychoanalysis (or, more loosely, psychology) where sociology usually stands.   *53*

   Such a position is only tenable if one accords a primacy
to internal (psychic) factors over external factors. This
thesis, which is systematically and rigorously integral to
Freudian thought, was actually subject to much uncertainty and many vacillations in his early work. A deeper
investigation might reveal *Totem and Taboo* as the work
which enabled Freud to focus on the meaning of con-
ceptualizing the primacy of internal factors over external
ones. This was the discovery of the psychic origins of
socio-cultural phenonema, although his concept of the
progressive internalization of social constraints left room
for several doubts, as we shall see. In an earlier paper,
'"Civilized" Sexual Morality and Modern Nervous Illness'(1908, *S.E.*, *9*), Freud tried to place the origins of
neurosis in social organization on to the demands of culture and education. He failed to take account of internal
conflict and tried to sever civilization from its individual
psychic roots. It is not surprising that Wilhelm Reich was
much taken with this and could not reconcile himself to

the fact that Freud abandoned these ideas. Reich went on to develop them himself.

But, as we mentioned earlier, even the thesis of *Totem and Taboo* (that the Oedipus complex lies at the basis of social organization) allows for the concept of the gradual phylogenetic transmission of what once were external constraints. This is clearly stated in a paper we have already cited, 'The Claims of Psychoanalysis to Scientific Interest' (which was published in the same year as *Totem and Taboo*), in which Freud points to the origins of 'the great cultural institutions' in 'primitive psychological situations', and to the predominance of sexual over social factors (*S.E.*, *13*, 185). The paragraph given to the discussion of 'The Sociological Interest of Psychoanalysis' contains Freud's suggestion that the internal demands of repression are related to the external demands of civilization when a neurosis is produced: just as 'a child who produces instinctual repressions spontaneously is merely repeating a part of the history of civilization. What is today an act of internal restraint was once an external one, imposed perhaps by the necessities of the moment' (189).

A great difference exists between this last statement and the thesis of '"Civilized" Sexual Morality', as the aetiology of the neuroses is no longer seen as being of purely external origin, but as the result of the relation between outside (environment) and inside (intrapsychic conflict). The paper never clearly establishes the primacy of internal factors, and remains contradictory over this. The equivocation, we feel, arises not only because of the inherent difficulty of this problem, which has preoccupied all sociology (whether Marxist or not) from its earliest

days, but also because of the importance that Freud
attached to basing the Oedipus complex on a real historic
event. The real event is the murder of the primal father by
the brothers of the horde. Alain Besançon has rightly
noted (personal communication) that the 'scientific myth'
of the primal horde has something of a defensive stance in
Freud's work. It seems to attribute the origin of individual experience, repeated afresh by every generation, to
'external' reality, to the real historic event. It requires
the hypothesis of phylogenetic memory traces which
transcend the experience of individual human beings.
Ultimately, it removes from the Oedipus complex its
characteristic of being an infantile conflict which, as we   55
outlined above, is painful and narcissistically wounding
because the oedipal wish is impossible to satisfy at the
time of the height of the Oedipus complex. The myth of
the primal horde and the murder of the father by the sons
who band up against him, the 'original sin' of the human
species, says Freud, gives the Oedipus complex a historical origin which takes away the responsibility of the
individual across generations, and ultimately reduces it to
being a conflict between adults. No doubt, there is much
that could be said about Freud's obstinate attachment to
the myth of the primal horde, and it seems likely that this
is one occasion on which the founder of psychoanalysis
had a resistance to being totally Freudian. However,
although psychoanalysing Freud is quite fashionable
these days, we feel it to be a sterile enterprise.

Adler once proposed the following objection: 'If you ask
where civilization comes from you are told "repression",
and if you ask where repression comes from you are told

"from civilization". So you see it is all simply playing with words.' In his paper 'On the History of the Psychoanalytic Movement', Freud counters this, saying:

> What is meant is simply that civilization is based on the repressions effected by former generations, and that each fresh generation is required to maintain this civilization by effecting the same repressions (1914, S.E., 14, 56–7).

Whereupon the founder of psychoanalysis invokes the old metaphor of the chicken and the egg. Yet in this work Freud has gone one step further. It is no longer a matter of phylogenetic inheritance, but one of a task which is renewed at each generation. Man is seen as being the starting-point of civilization, and, even if this is not referring to the contemporary human subject, it certainly does mean the human ancestral lineage. We resemble our forbears a great deal, having many structures in common. So no one could say that Freud's development towards the concept of the primacy of internal factors was a straightforward one. But we have shown that, despite many vacillations, his emphasis was always on unconscious psychic conflict. In one sense this is what constitutes the specificity of psychoanalysis *vis-à-vis* all other psychologies.

It may be useful to recall one of Freud's ideas on repression, according to which it is a mechanism of organic origin:

> One gets the impression from civilized children that the construction of these dams is a product of education, and no doubt education has much to do with it. But in reality this development is organically determined and

fixed by heredity, and it can occasionally occur without any help at all from education (1905, *S.E.*, *7*, 177–8).

As early as 1897, in a letter to Fliess, Freud had written: 'I have often suspected that something organic played a part in repression' (Freud, 1954, 231).

A study of Freud's ideas on the mutual relations between the 'internal' and the 'external' as concepts on the relation between the individual and society would be very useful. Such a study might compare '"Civilized" Sexual Morality' from 1908 and *Civilization and its Discontents* from 1930. James Strachey, who translated the English language editions of Freud's work and who added an excellent critical commentary to them, confirms our own view when he writes in the introduction to the second of these texts:

> No analysis of the deeper, internal origins of civilization is to be found in what is by far the longest of Freud's earlier discussions of the subject, his paper on '"Civilized" Sexual Morality and Modern Nervous Illness', which gives the impression of the restrictions of civilization as something imposed from without (*S.E.*, *21*, 61).

It was actually the introduction of the second topography, with the division of the psychic apparatus into three agencies, the id, the ego and the superego, as well as the concomitant introduction of the death instinct, that brought about a new formulation of the relations between the individual and civilization. We might add that the date of Freud's writing of *Civilization and its Discontents* is not insignificant, taking into account the economic crisis in America, the first effects of which were being felt in

Europe, and the fact that Germany was suffering the birth pangs of Nazism. According to Reich, *Civilization and its Discontents* was also written 'specifically in response to one of my lectures in Freud's home. I was the one who was *"unbehaglich in der Kultur"*' (Reich, 1952, 44).

In this context we can only pursue a few of the points that Freud raises in this work. The book is presented as a meditation on happiness. Curiously enough, if Reich considered it to be a (negative) response to his ideas (and in 1932 he refuted the concept of the death drive), Marcuse – whose work is not really under discussion here and who will only be mentioned in passing – (there are two chapters on the subject of Marcuse in Stéphane (1969)) makes extensive use of the book and manages to annexe it for his own arguments by an intellectual sleight of hand. We could either, generously, attribute this to his dexterity, or else to the inadequacy of his reading of Freud, as well as his complete lack of any experience of psychoanalysis, which he admits to in an interview (*L'Express*, 23 September 1968, No. 898).

In fact, Freud is writing about man's difficulty in finding happiness, despite the undeniable advances made by civilization. Man yearns for satisfaction; before the differentiation of ego and object, the pleasure principle is the absolute dictator of the psychic apparatus. The pleasure principle has a free flow of psychic energy. Frustrations bring about the differentiation between the ego and non-ego (object, outside world), and a progressive differentiation between the ego (as an agency) and the id.

If the id's instinctual demands meet with no satisfaction, intolerable conditions arise. Experience soon shows that these situations of satisfaction can only be established with the help of the external world. At that point the portion of the id which is directed towards the external world – the ego – begins to function. If all the driving force that sets the vehicle in motion is derived from the id, the ego, as it were, undertakes the steering, without which no goal can be reached. The instincts in the id press for immediate satisfaction at all costs, and in that way they achieve nothing or even bring about appreciable damage. It is the task of the ego to guard against such mishaps, to mediate between the claims of the id and the objections of the external world. It carries on its activity in two directions. On the one hand, it observes the external world with its sense-organ, the systems of consciousness, so as to catch the favourable moment for harmless satisfaction; and on the other hand it influences the id, bridles its passions, induces its instincts to postpone their satisfaction, and indeed, if the necessity is recognized, to modify its aims, or, in return for some compensation, to give them up. In so far as it tames the id's impulses in this way, it replaces the pleasure principle, which was formerly alone decisive, by what is known as the 'reality principle', which, though it pursues the same ultimate aims, takes into account the conditions imposed by the real external world . . . The differentiation of an ego is above all a step towards self-preservation (1926, *S.E.*, *20*, 200–2).

59

Marcuse's misreading is simple: he assimilates the 'reality principle' to a 'performance principle' and imagines a world in which this principle would, ultimately, vanish. In other words, he posits a world in which unconscious-

ness and undifferentiation would reign, but this, as Freud
has shown, would only lead to death. The major obstacle
to happiness is the very nature of the pleasure principle,
the free, unbounded flow of psychic energy, which, even if
it were actualized, could not result in happiness. Happiness presupposes the existence of the reality principle, as
Freud writes in *Civilization and its Discontents*:

> What we call happiness in the strict sense comes from
> the (preferably sudden) satisfaction of needs which
> have been dammed up to a high degree, and it is from
> its nature only possible as a periodic phenomenon.
> When any situation that is desired by the pleasure
> principle is prolonged it only produces a feeling of mild
> contentment. We are so made that we can derive
> intense enjoyment only from a contrast and very little
> from a state of things. Thus our possibilities of happi-
> ness are already restricted by our constitution (1930,
> *S.E.*, *21*, 76).

So, it is the coexistence of the bound energy of the reality
principle, along with the pleasure principle, which produces pleasure. Pleasure is, by definition, ephemeral as it
requires an accumulation of energy in order to give the
discharge its intensity. Again, Marcuse makes a confusion
between pleasure and the pleasure principle. Freud
clearly states that the (relative) replacement of the
pleasure principle by the reality principle is not done
primarily in the interests of civilization but in the interests
of self-preservation. It is this replacement alone which
makes possible the fleeting moments of happiness known
to man.

But man's search for happiness can take more modest

and indirect forms – by diminishing the unpleasant aspects of life – which the reality principle and the ego make possible:

> Another technique for fending off suffering is the employment of the displacements of the libido which our mental apparatus permits of and through which its function gains so much inflexibility. The task here is that of shifting the instinctual aims in such a way that they cannot come up against frustration from the external world. In this, sublimation of the instincts lends its assistance. One gains the most if one can sufficiently heighten the yield of pleasure from the sources of psychical and intellectual work. When that is so, fate can do little against one. A satisfaction of this kind, such as an artist's joy in creating, in giving his phantasies body, or a scientist's in solving problems or discovering truths, has a special quality which we shall certainly one day be able to characterize in metapsychological terms (79).

61

Freud acknowledges that the special quality of these satisfactions is of a lesser intensity than that of those produced by the direct satisfaction of an instinct. However, far from considering the process of sublimation in work as 'surplus repression' (Marcuse, 1966, 35) he adds, in a footnote:

> When there is no special disposition in a person which imperatively prescribes what direction his interests in life shall take, the ordinary professional work that is open to everyone can play the part assigned to it in *Candide*, to cultivate one's garden, Voltaire's wise advice. It is not possible, within the limits of a short

survey, to discuss adequately the significance of work for the economics of the libido . . . The possibility it offers of displacing a large amount of libidinal components, whether narcissistic, aggressive, or even erotic, on to professional work and on to the human relations connected with it lends a value by no means second to what it enjoys as something indispensable to the preservation and justification of existence in society. Professional activity is a source of special satisfaction if it is a freely chosen one – if, that is to say, by means of sublimation, it makes possible the use of existing inclinations, of persisting or constitutionally reinforced instinctual impulses (60).

Whilst it is clear that the conditions most favourable to the sublimation of instincts are those in which one's profession is freely chosen, this is nevertheless a far call from the idea that all work is total 'alienation' without pleasure, as Marcuse would have it. Marcuse claims to be inspired by Freud and yet also claims that any pleasure one may derive from work is either illusory or a further sign of alienation:

Certainly there can be 'pleasure' in alienated labour too. The typist who hands in a perfect typescript, the tailor who delivers a perfectly fitting suit, the beauty parlour attendant who fixes the perfect hairdo, the labourer who fulfils his daily quota – all may feel pleasure in a 'job well done'. However, either this pleasure is extraneous (anticipation of reward), or it is the satisfaction (itself a token of repression) of being well occupied, in the right place, of contributing one's part to the functioning of the apparatus (Marcuse, 220).

After reviewing the diverse ways available to man to attenuate his suffering, if not to achieve happiness, Freud goes on to compare the 'process of civilization' to 'normal maturation of the individual'. In a lengthy footnote he speculates about the consequences of our transition to an upright posture, the 'verticalization' which, according to Freud, triggered off the 'fateful process of civilization'. This transition entailed the repression of certain anal satisfactions and led to such phenomena as hygiene, orderliness and cleanliness which are closely bound to cultural development. 'Thus anal eroticism succumbs first,' says Freud, to this 'organic repression which opens the path to civilization.' This civilizing process must have   *63* been set off by an internal factor. This hypothesis of Freud's had previously been the subject of many debates which started in 1897, in his letters to Fliess. According to Freud, the anal factor and its reaction formations play a fundamental role in the process of civilization.

Civilization places constraints on the sexual life of mankind, and thus on one of the possibilities for obtaining the most intense happiness. In this case, happiness is constrained by our dependence on the love object, but, in addition, civilization tends to channel a certain amount of sexual energy towards the interests of work and culture, and to stipulate the conditions for its release:

> As regards the sexually mature individual, the choice of an object is restricted to the opposite sex, and most extra-genital satisfactions are forbidden as perversions. The requirement, demonstrated in these prohibitions, that there shall be a single kind of sexual life for everyone, disregards the dissimilarities, whether innate or

acquired, in the sexual constitution of human beings; it cuts off a fair number of them from sexual enjoyment, and so becomes the source of a serious injustice. The result of such restrictive measures might be that in people who are normal – who are not prevented by their constitution – the whole of their sexual interests would flow without loss into the channels that are left open. But heterosexual genital love, which has remained exempt from outlawry, is itself restricted by further limitations, in the shape of insistence on legitimacy and monogamy. Present-day civilization makes it plain that it will only permit sexual relationships on the basis of a solitary, indissoluble bond between one man and one woman, and that it does not like sexuality as a source of pleasure in its own right, and is only prepared to tolerate it because there is so far no substitute for it as a means of propagating the human race (*S.E.*, *21*, 104–5).

64

The passage quoted above has had a special fate. It has been made into the justification for many Marcusian (and leftist) revindications of perversion against monogamy, and the basis for thinking of genital activity as a veritable duty. Marcuse 'rejects the normal Eros in favour of a more complete Eros', and 'protests against the order of procreative sexuality'. Perversions are the 'symbol of identity, freedom and happiness'. But this passage of Freud's can only be properly understood in its context. In the dialectical form, which is a feature of this book, the constraints on sexuality which are here seen as imposed by civilization are later attributed to internal factors:

Sometimes one seems to perceive that it is not only the pressure of civilization but something in the nature of the [sexual] function itself which denies us full satisfaction and urges us along other paths [followed by a long footnote supporting this hypothesis] (105).

This also corresponds to the idea that Freud developed earlier in his essay 'On the Universal Tendency to Debasement in the Sphere of Love' (1912):

> It is my belief that, however strange it may sound, we must reckon with the possibility that something in the nature of the sexual instinct itself is unfavourable to the realization of complete satisfaction (*S.E.*, *11*, 188–9).

It is, basically, a problem of the subsisting oedipal wishes which cannot be satisfied except through a substitute for the real object of desire. Freud also noted that:

65

> Man's discovery of sexual (genital) love afforded him the strongest experiences of satisfaction, and in fact provided him with the prototype of all happiness (*S.E.*, *21*, 101).

Furthermore, in *Group Psychology and the Analysis of the Ego* (1921) Freud shows the development of monogamy, as it was perfectly compatible with the nature of the sexual aim on one hand, and with emotional love on the other:

> In the history of the development of the family there have also, it is true, been group relations of sexual love (group marriages); but the more important sexual love became for the ego, and the more it developed the characteristics of being in love, the more urgently it required to be limited to two people – *una cum uno* – as it is prescribed by the nature of the genital aim. Poly-

gamous inclinations had to be content to find satisfaction in a succession of changing objects.

Two people coming together for the purpose of sexual satisfaction, in so far as they seek for solitude, are making a demonstration against the herd instinct, the group feeling. The more they are in love, the more completely they suffice for each other . . . It is only when the affectionate, that is, the personal, factor of a love relation gives place entirely to the sensual one, that it is possible for two people to have sexual intercourse in the presence of others or for there to be simultaneous sexual acts in a group, as occurs at an orgy. But at that point a regression has taken place to an early stage in sexual relations, at which being in love as yet played no part, and all sexual objects were judged to be of equal value, somewhat in the sense of Bernard Shaw's malicious aphorism to the effect that being in love means greatly exaggerating the difference between one woman and another (*S.E.*, *18*, 140).

66

(This regression is to be understood as reaching back to the anal stage, when all objects are completely interchangeable, just as faeces are identical, whereas at the oedipal stage the object is completely individualized: it is *him* my father, or *her* my mother that I want, and nobody else.)

This is less a case of contradictory thinking on Freud's part than one of his adopting a different approach to the same problem. On the one hand, civilization pushes us towards monogamy, which will be a constraint for some (regressive) individuals; on the other hand, individual maturation tends spontaneously towards monogamy. Thus,

civilization tends to promote those institutions which
cater only for the apex of individual development. This
rather subtle idea is not an argument for group marriage;
love isolates, 'whereas civilization depends on relationships between a considerable number of individuals'.[3]

The main cause of the conflict between the instincts and
civilization comes from the fact that 'men are not gentle
creatures who want to be loved, and who at most can
defend themselves if they are attacked; they are, on the
contrary, creatures among whose instinctual endowments
is to be reckoned a powerful share of aggressiveness'. Man
is, in fact, a wolf to man, says Freud, and it is this
'inclination to aggression . . . which forces civilization
into such a high expenditure of energy'. Human nature is
such, and the efforts of civilization to control aggression
are so rarely successful that 'each one of us has to give up
as illusions the expectations which, in his youth, he
pinned upon his fellow men . . .' Whereupon Freud again
criticizes the Communists' faith in human benevolence:
the abolition of private property can never result in the
eradication of human malignity. Aggression is in man, not
just in the institutions.

As we know, civilization actually offers us some degree
of protection from the aggression of others: 'In fact, primitive man was better off in knowing no restrictions of
instinct. To counterbalance this, his prospects of enjoying
this happiness for any length of time were very slender.
Civilized man has exchanged a portion of his possibilities
of happiness for a portion of security.' Furthermore, the
customs of some contemporary 'primitive' societies suggest that the members of early societies 'were subject to

67

restrictions of another order, more severe perhaps than
those endured by modern society'.

So we must abandon any hope of ever returning to a
totally mythical Golden Age. In any case, Freud's work is
a repudiation of Illusion, especially the illusion of alternative societies, and the illusion of the overthrow of the
process of civilization which is part of the process of
humanization. We have no choice. The alternative to
civilization is not the pastoral idyll but barbarism. Freud
declares, 'We are not showing ourselves [to be] enemies of
civilization' (*S.E.*, *21*, 115).

Freud concludes *Civilization and its Discontents* by introducing the concept of the death drive, an autonomous
instinct of aggression. Civilization serves Eros which
guarantees the survival of the species, and which is in
conflict with the death drive. Eros tends towards unifica-
tion, whereas aggression tends towards fragmentation.
(Clearly, though, the opposition is not between Eros and
civilization, which again shows how Freud's view is different from Marcuse's.) Freud proceeds to inquire into
the way in which aggression is controlled by civilization.
He describes how aggression is inhibited, is turned back,
by the subject, towards himself. This is the formation of
the superego, which acts as an internal monitor of the
subject's ego. At first, the feeling of guilt was an expression of our anxiety towards external authorities such as
parents (and their substitutes), and this now becomes
what the ego feels in relation to the superego. Earlier we
mentioned how civilization was conceptualized as being
in the service of Eros, but Freud's later conception shows
how this process entails the cultivation of the death drive,
aggression which is turned back in on the subject's own

68

self. Whereas the fulfilment of certain wishes might result in anxiety *vis-à-vis* authorities, the wishes themselves are enough to elicit anxiety *vis-à-vis* the omniscient superego. In fact, the more we renounce our wishes and drives, the more pronounced becomes the severity of the superego: 'Every piece of aggression whose satisfaction the subject gives up is taken over by the superego and increases the latter's aggressiveness.' So every instinctual renunciation, or frustration of whatever order which was originally enforced by an external authority, elicits intense aggression, which love for this same authority forces the subject to internalize, thus reinforcing the severity of the superego.

69

According to Freud, the sense of guilt originated in a real event: the murder of the father of the primal horde. Guilt expresses the remorse inherent in the resurgence of love felt for the father once the sons' hatred had been satiated. The sons internalized the dead father's authority in the form of the superego. The sense of guilt, however, remains partly unconscious, being linked to unfulfilled wishes, which are also unconscious. So the feeling of guilt that is provoked by civilization cannot be recognized as such, and is felt as discontentment.

Freud considers the sense of guilt to be the most significant problem in the development of civilization: 'the price we pay for our advance in civilization is the loss of happiness through the heightening of the sense of guilt'. When Freud compares the evolution of society to the development of the individual, to show the part played by the superego in discontentment, we feel there is one aspect of this which is particularly relevant today. In a footnote, referring to some of Alexander's ideas, he suggests (*S.E.*,

21, 130) that the severity of the superego can result from two different factors – either from the parents being too strict or from their being too lenient. In the latter case, the child who has been too much indulged has no resource other than to turn back his aggression on to his own ego.

The title of Freud's book, *Civilization and its Discontents*, relates two completely interdependent terms. It is naive to imagine, as some people do, that these could be separated and that there could be a civilization without discontent. In the book Freud writes: '. . . we may also familiarize ourselves with the idea that there are difficulties attaching to the nature of civilization which will not yield to any attempt at reform' (115).

The concept of the death drive is rejected by many analysts; even Freud described it as a 'hypothesis of so fantastic a kind – a myth rather than a scientific explanation' (*Beyond the Pleasure Principle*; 1920, *S.E.*, *18*, 57). One might think that to reject the concept of the death drive undermines the entire foundation of *Civilization and its Discontents*. But if we reject the idea that 'aggression is an autonomous and instinctual primary characteristic of the human being' which is the most formidable opponent of civilization, this does not alter Freud's basic conclusions. We feel, and we are not the only ones, that it is possible to accept the existence of instinctual aggression without giving this the significance that Freud gave the death drive – that of the biological law of the tendency of matter to revert to an inorganic state. From its earliest days Freudian theory acknowledged the existence of aggressive drives, in the concept of ambivalence, the coexistence of love and hate. They are also implicated in the Oedipus complex in the death wishes towards the parent of the

70

same sex. We cannot believe in the naive Rousseauistic theory that aggression is merely a reaction to frustration, and that human beings could be at peace with themselves and with others in a society which had abolished frustration. Even if one accepts the idea that aggression is only a response to frustration, it must be remembered that frustration is inherent in the human condition.

Human prematurity means that frustration is inevitable and leads the ego to differentiate itself from the non-ego, the subject to separate itself from the object. 'Indeed, the primal narcissistic state would not be able to develop it if were not for the fact that every individual passes through a period . . . during which his pressing needs are satisfied by an external agency' (1915, *S.E.*, *14*, 135).

71

As it is precisely this frustration which enables the subject to recognize the object, the latter, according to Freud, is born of hatred. Even if the concept of innate aggression is rejected, the human condition of prematurity means that if aggression emerges independently from objective reality (mother, the environment, or society) it is fateful for the subject. In the same way, any discussion of the death drive can only, psychoanalytically speaking, be applied to the 'metaphysical' significance of this concept. The death drive in man has to be 'deflected' towards the outside world so that the subject does not remain its victim, so that the subject avoids self-destruction. It should be remembered that Freud himself, when introducing the concept of the death drive, said:

> If such an assumption as this is permissible, then we have met the demand that we should produce an example of a death instinct – though, it is true, a very displaced one. But this way of looking at things is very

far from easy to grasp and creates a positively mystical impression (*Beyond the Pleasure Principle*; 1921, *S.E.*, *18*, 54).

And also:

> It may be asked whether and how far I am myself convinced of the truth of the hypotheses that have been set out in these pages. My answer would be that I am not convinced myself and that I do not seek to persuade other people to believe in them. Or, more precisely, that I do not know how far I believe in them. There is no reason, as it seems to me, why the emotional factor of conviction should enter into this question at all. It is surely possible to throw oneself into a line of thought and to follow it wherever it leads out of simple scientific curiosity, or, if the reader prefers, as a devil's advocate, who is not on that account himself sold to the devil. I do not dispute the fact that the third step in the theory of the instincts, which I have taken here, cannot lay claim to the same degree of certainty as the two earlier ones – the extension of the concept of sexuality and the hypothesis of narcissism (59).

In *Civilization and its Discontents*, Freud is more positive:

> To begin with it was only tentatively that I put forward the views I have developed here, but in the course of time they have gained such a hold upon me that I can no longer think in any other way . . . I can no longer understand how we overlooked the ubiquity of non-erotic aggressivity and destructiveness and can have failed to give it its due place in our interpretation of life.

72

For 'little children do not like it' when there is talk of the inborn human inclination to 'badness', to aggressiveness, destructiveness and so to cruelty as well (119–20).

However, towards the end of his life Freud's doubts about the 'strange hypothesis' of the death instinct returned to him, as we see in his letters to Marie Bonaparte on the subject:

> The turning inward of the aggressive impulse is naturally the counterpart of turning outward of the libido when it passes over from the ego to objects. One could imagine a pretty schematic idea of all libido being at the beginning of life directed inward and all aggression outward, and that this gradually changes in the course of life. But perhaps that is not correct.

And also:

> Please do not overestimate my remarks about the destructive instinct. They were only tossed off and should be carefully thought over if you propose to use them publicly. Also there is little new in them (Jones, 464–5).

In neither case is it a question of denying the innate aggression in man, nor that this aggression is indissolubly linked with specific prematurity. Nor is it, except for the 'little children' who 'do not like it', a question of imagining that any social transformation might eradicate human aggression. We cannot claim that aggression derives from specific historical conjunctures. It is always present, in latent form, and external conditions can activate it to a greater or lesser degree, but can neither create nor destroy

73

it. No changes in the material conditions of existence can efface the narcissistic blow dealt to the infant by its condition of prematurity and the Oedipus complex. Even if, hypothetically, the incest taboo could be eradicated, the Oedipus complex could not, because of the anachronism between the oedipal child's wishes and its capacity to satisfy those wishes, which would still exist. Thus it is clear that, for Freudian psychoanalysis, internal factors play a primary role. Civilization itself is seen as the result of the conflict between primary drives and the defences against those drives. It is surely not arbitrary that Freud comes to express, very clearly, his view of the primacy of internal, psychic, over external factors with reference to Marxism:

74

> The strength of Marxism clearly lies, not in its view of history or the prophecies of the future that are based on it, but in its sagacious indication of the decisive influence which the economic circumstances of man have upon their intellectual, ethical, and artistic attitudes. A number of connections and implications were thus uncovered, which had previously been almost totally overlooked. But it cannot be assumed that economic motives are the only ones that determine the behaviour of human beings in society . . . It is altogether incomprehensible how psychological factors can be overlooked where what is in question are the reactions of living human beings; for not only were these reactions concerned in establishing the economic conditions, but even under the domination of those conditions men can only bring their original instinctual impulses into play – their self-preservative instinct,

their aggressiveness, their need to be loved, their drive towards obtaining pleasure and avoiding unpleasure (1932, *S.E.*, *22*, 178).

We think it is important to make a connection between the phenomenon of the transference and the internal psychic factors underlying the ensemble of human activities and behaviour. Freud referred to the transference throughout his work and devoted a whole paper to it, in which he notes that it is a manifestation of a much more general process (1912, *S.E.*, *12*, 57). We can see this process at work in certain stereotypes which are repeated time and again, and are lived out in life. Only a fraction of infantile libidinal wishes actually reach full psychic maturity; 'this part is directed towards reality, is part of the conscious self and is under its control'. Meanwhile, the other parts of the libidinal wishes remain separate from the conscious self and from reality, and may follow either of two paths. Either these wishes can be satisfied on the level of fantasy, or else they may remain entirely unconscious, entirely withdrawn from the conscious self. If the subject's need for love has not been completely satisfied in reality, the subject is led to approach every new encounter with the expectation of having these wishes satisfied. The cathexis of these objects works according to prototypes, clichés, stereotypes, imaginary schemata. It is the parental imagos that will be materialized in the subject's relation to his objects. (An imago is 'an unconscious prototypical figure which orientates the subject's way of apprehending others; it is built up on the basis of the first real and phantasied relationships within the family environment' (Laplanche & Pontalis, 1973).) When these imagos are

75

projected on to the analyst in the course of analysis they are all the more easy to notice because the analytic context (the fundamental rule of free association, the analyst's place behind the subject, who thus cannot see him, and the neutrality of the analyst, which implies the absence of a real relationship with the analysand) not only facilitates the emergence of these imagos but also enables them to be pared down and acknowledged in their original purity, which in turn makes it possible to analyse them. But 'It must not be supposed, however, that transference is created by analysis and does not occur apart from it. Transference is merely uncovered and isolated by analysis. It is a universal phenomenon of the human mind . . . and in fact dominates the whole of each person's relations to his human environment' (1925, *S.E.*, *20*, 42).

76

The concept of transference, as a universal human phenomenon, implies that beneath all human behaviour we will find the earliest, most fundamental relationships of a subject to his or her first objects. Our real life objects are, at least in part, a repetition, or new edition, of our first objects. We transfer on to our butcher, cashier, employee, boss. This doesn't necessarily mean that the whole relation is taken over by the parental imago, nor that the object's reaction has no effect on the relationship between himself and the subject. If this were true we would all be living in the realm of illusions. It simply means that the present-day relationship will reawaken unfulfilled wishes from the past (both libidinal and aggressive), and because of this fact it will contain certain irrational elements. As has been stated, there are a number of elements that exist in the unconscious, universally, independently of personal history, and it is thus possible to uncover the infan-

tile roots of some group behaviour. It can then be seen as
being still under the influence, to varying extents of
course, of unfulfilled infantile wishes displaced on to figures in the present.

The mechanism of symbolization also bears some relation to the transference. For example, the need to find
substitutes for the prohibited objects of incest is what
facilitates symbol formation. Whilst Freud did not really
provide us with a foolproof theory of symbolic activity, he
repeatedly showed (whilst asking the reader to forgive the
monotony of psychoanalytic interpretations) the infinite
number of symbols when compared to the small number
of things that are symbolized.

77

In the *Introductory Lectures on Psychoanalysis* (1917), he
claims that the essence of symbolism is in the comparison
between the symbol and the thing symbolized (comparison of form, size, etc.). The material symbolized is limited
to parents, brothers, sisters, bodily organs and in particular the erogenous zones, coitus and castration. The concept of primal fantasies, described above, and certain
'typical dreams' where conflict is represented in a stereotyped form (independently of the personal history of the
dreamer), show the universality of some symbols. It was
Ferenczi who started to describe the genesis of symbolic
activity whilst accounting for how narrow the range of
material symbolized is when compared to the innumerable symbols, and the universal nature of these:

> . . . children concern themselves to begin with only
> about the satisfactions of their instincts, i.e. about the
> parts of the body where this satisfaction takes place,
> about the objects suited to evoke this, and about the

actions that actually evoke the satisfaction. Of the sexually excitable parts of the body (erogenous zones), for instance, they are especially interested in the mouth, the anus and the genitals. What wonder then, if also his attention is arrested above all by those objects and processes of the outer world that on the ground of ever so distant a resemblance remind him of his dearest experiences? (Ferenczi, 1913, 276).

From this text we may deduce that knowledge of the outside world starts from the subject's own body and that the formation of symbols consists of a projection on to external space, which thus comes to be, on one level, an extension of the body. (This process is not unrelated to the animism and magic of so-called primitive societies; and it can also be compared to the confusion between the body and nature, physiological acts and the elements in schizophrenia, for example in the *Autobiography of a Schizophrenic Girl* (1950), Marguerite Séchéhaye writes of a patient who confuses urination and rain.)

78

Melanie Klein links symbol-formation to the anxiety felt in the fears of retaliation from the part-objects (breasts, penis) about which the child has destructive fantasies. This anxiety pushes the child to find equivalents for these objects and the symbolic process of substitution gradually extends itself to the outside world (Klein, 1929).

In both of these theories of symbolic activity it is the primary objects which undergo a process of displacement so that the relation between subject and outside world bears the indelible stamp of the archaic prototypes on which it was based. This is the way in which symboliza-

tion is similar to the transference, and this is the way that
the subject's relation to the world is forever coloured by
psychobiological factors. The International Congress of
Psychoanalysis, which was held in Paris in 1973, had on
its agenda a round-table discussion on the transference. It
was a pity that the distinguished analysts around the table
contented themselves with repeating hackneyed notions
about the role of the transference in therapy without once
mentioning that 'the transference is a universal phenomenon of the human mind', to be strictly Freudian. Nor
did they try to come to terms with the consequences of this
fact.

It is true, and it cannot be said too often, that the
concepts of the transference and symbolization inevitably
make psychoanalysis reductive, as is any system of interpretation. Marxism too, in reducing morality, philosophy, religion, art and ideas to the relations and forces of
production, is reductive. And those ideologies which
claim to be interpretations or decodings of social reality,
aren't they reductive too? To interpret is to give something a meaning and thus to reduce the multiplicity and
complexity of phenomena to a common denominator,
which allows us to uncover a structure based on a mini-
mum number of causes and, in the last analysis, on one
factor which is the prevalent cause if not the only one.

Freud wrote that 'the theory of symbolization has cost
psychoanalysis many enemies'. Clearly the process of
reducing the most subtle, sublime and apparently freest
elaborations of the human mind to their (ludicrous) infantile prototypes entails a blow to narcissism, a humiliation,
that psychoanalysis will not easily be forgiven. Psychoanalysts are particularly sensitive to the accusation of

'reductionism' which is frequently directed at those who venture beyond the limits of clinical practice. Analysts are always dealing with the castration complex and this accusation of 'reductionism' has resonances for them which never fail to make them feel guilty. They would rather be inconsistent with themselves, ignoring whole sections of Freud's work, than be attacked. Freud wrote: 'I have long recognized that to stir up contradiction and arouse bitterness is the inevitable fate of psychoanalysis' (1914, *S.E.*, *14*, 8). The problem is that the contradiction affects psychoanalysts themselves. And yet, without reduction no *clinical or theoretical* work in even the most 80 specialized medical field is possible in psychoanalysis. This is not only because interpretation is inherently reductive, but because all scientific work in psycho-analysis, as in other disciplines, means deducing certain general rules and thus reducing the complexity, fluidity and heterogeneity of reality to an indivisible and perma-nent core. From the moment when an analyst claims to be studying depression, hysteria, perversion, schizophrenia, he reduces all those people – the depressed, the hysterics, perverts, and schizophrenics – to the common denomina-tor characteristic of those illnesses. In so doing, the ana-lyst is obeying the rules of scientific work.

Because of this it is impossible to make a qualitative difference between the clinical practice of a psychoanalyst and his non-therapeutic research. It is contradictory to accept psychoanalysis as a therapeutic process whilst refusing its interpretations of general human phenomena. It is admissible, of course, to question a particular inter-pretation, as is the case in clinical studies, but it is contra-dictory to claim, as do certain Marxists, both that psychoanalysis can explain depression *and* that its theory of the innate aggression of man is simply an expression of nineteenth-century bourgeois ideology. The interpretation of depression (and other mental states) is based on this theory of aggression. And any claim which is inapplicable to mankind in general cannot be viably applied to one man in particular just because he happens to be lying on a psychoanalyst's couch. It is impossible to put a patient 'in parentheses'.

In fact, the boundaries between therapeutic psychoanalysis and its non-clinical applications are far from clear or settled. When it is claimed that female sexuality can only be understood in terms of the social position of women, this amounts to a prohibition of working with women in the analytic context. A psychoanalytic approach to the question of the social position of women seeks to explain it by examining the drives and their defences in both men and women, especially in relation to the mother. By the same token, it would also be impossible to use the analytic method on male subjects as femininity is a constitutive element of human sexuality in general. It is surprising, then, that some analysts are being carried away by fashion and popular consensus, and are trying to explain female sexuality in terms of social and economic conditions. The most basic concern for consistency and integrity would require them to stop practising a profession in which they no longer believe (unless they are victims of an astonishingly split personality). And as for the infamous 'reductionism', isn't this mainly being carried out by those who try to constrain analysis to the consulting room? All that would remain of Freud's vast project, from his ambition to 'understand something of the riddles of the world', would be the vestiges of a therapeutic practice.

We now want to reply to an objection that is often made to extra-therapeutic psychoanalytic interpretations. It is often claimed that such interpretations are based on a very few constants, such as the Oedipus complex, which are incapable of encompassing the endless variety of human activities. A Freudian analyst would reply by referring to the two concepts outlined above, the transference and symbolization. Due to the processes they share, these concepts make it possible to find a limited number of primary objects beneath a multiplicity of signs and relationships which appear to be very far removed from the original matrices. Our imaginary analyst might then turn the objection back on to the critic (a Marxist, for example), asking him to account for the repetitive and stereotyped nature of, say, antisemitic projections through the centuries, despite great differences in historical conjunctures. He might also ask him, politely, to come up with an analysis of Nazism which goes beyond the classic, but unconvincing, analysis which says it is just one of the vicissitudes of capitalism. An explanation of the events of May 1968 which could account for the role played by middle-class youth would also be welcome.

But our Freudian analyst should not content himself with looking for the primary drives and the Oedipus complex underlying diverse human phenomena – the sociopolitical, for example. It is also essential to find the precipitating factor (such as the 'trigger action' in a neurosis) and to relate this to the latent contents of the unconscious which were thus activated. For example, a humiliation (a blow to narcissism) in conjunction with material and physical impoverishment (defeat), to which are added more frustrations (inflation, unemployment, poverty), can also activate a terrifying archaic imago and a need for intense illusion. If man had no unconscious imagos his external circumstances would have no effect. The conjunction of internal factors and a given historical context is required for otherwise latent or suppressed drives to manifest themselves.

Furthermore, if the Oedipus complex is universal and thus is likely to be found in all cultural activities, the psychoanalyst must nevertheless go beyond finding the traces of its structure in whatever happens to be the object of his study. For the *solutions* to the Oedipus complex are   83 multiple and are infinitely varied. And one of these solutions, for reasons to be linked with the precipitating factor, will tend to predominate. It is the specificity of the solution that must be unearthed.

Finally, as we shall see, although the human psyche is structured by certain universals, mankind is nonetheless capable of progress, within specific limits. In fact, one of these universals, the Oedipus complex and the prematurity on which it is based, pushes successive generations to surpass preceding generations. Note that 'progress' tends to be most visible in the fields of science and technology. Might it be as some belated attempt to compensate for man's motor incapacity in the earliest years of his life, his original helplessness, that he builds and uses these fabulous machines? Why is it only one sector of humanity that has become involved in technology? These are questions that ethnologist-psychoanalysts could add to their research agenda. In any case, it seems that the mechanical universe within which man is evolving acts in turn to trigger off certain wishes and fantasies. To the extent that they can awaken dormant psychical phenomena, material conditions are not without effect in the psyche.

There is an important corollary to this emphasis on psychical (internal) factors, that is, a scepticism, if not pessimism, in politics. Freud always found himself in retreat from all types of extremism. His position, at least on Communism, is evident not only in his publications but also in anecdotes and in his personal correspondence. Ernest Jones remembers a conversation with Freud in 1919:

84

> There were, of course, comments on the vast changes in the European situation, and Freud surprised me by saying he had recently had an interview with an ardent Communist and had been half-converted to Bolshevism, as it was then called. He had been informed that the advent of Bolshevism would result in some years of misery and chaos, and that these would be followed by universal peace, prosperity and happiness. Freud added: 'I told him I believed the first half' (Jones, 16).

In his correspondence with Arnold Zweig the letter of 26 November 1930 again reveals Freud's political position. Arnold Zweig was, unlike Freud, ardently political and had sent the latter a manifesto for his signature. Freud's reply is unambiguous:

> I would give it gladly, did not the manifesto contain an attack on 'the capitalist economic confusion'. For that would be tantamount to giving my support to the Communist ideal, and I am far from wishing to do that. In

spite of all my dissatisfaction with the present economic system I have no hope that the road pursued by the Soviets will lead to improvement. Indeed any such hope that I may have cherished has disappeared in this decade of Soviet rule. I remain a liberal of the old school. In my last book I criticized uncompromisingly the mixture of despotism and Communism [*Civilization and its Discontents*]. I do not know whether the Russian dictators pay any attention to the utterances of a few 'intellectuals' – probably they do not give a brass farthing for them – but if they do, then the effect of the manifesto could only be damaged by the signature of a declared opponent like myself (21–2).

85

Freud's political opinions are usually explained in terms of his social origins. We think it necessary, on the contrary, to emphasize the close link that exists between Freud's attitude to politics and the discovery of the unconscious; that is, psychoanalysis itself. This attitude, in other words, stems from psychoanalysis and is in keeping with the Freudian conception of the psyche, particularly the theories of the instincts and the Oedipus complex. And if one were to identify some characteristic of Freud's personality that might have inflected his choices in one direction rather than another, it should be remembered that it was this very personality which was at the heart of the revolutionary discovery of psychoanalysis.

But if the facts are to be known, remember that Freud was born in Moravia in Freiberg (today a Czech town called Příbor). Sigmund's father, Jakob, a wool merchant of Jewish origin, was hard-pressed to raise his large family. Sigmund was the oldest son of his father's second marriage (he had seven children after Sigmund and two from his first marriage). Jakob and his wife Amalia settled in Vienna following the collapse of his business. Once in Vienna Jakob's business did not improve, and the family were constantly on the brink of poverty, sometimes very poor. The parents made heroic efforts for their children to obtain higher education. All things considered, Freud's family background was that of the lower middle class in financial difficulty. Sigmund Freud later came to lead the ordered life of a family man – initially on a very modest financial level. His revolution was entirely on the level of ideas. The reduction of the courage and substance of Freud's discovery to considerations of his social origins is the product of a 'vulgar' Marxism, of a mentality which is fundamentally reactionary (in the sense of refusing to question the received ideas of a prefabricated intellectual framework). Alternatively, this game could be played out to its logical conclusions and it could be noted that Marx came from a background that was even more bourgeois than Freud's.

Without going into every detail of Marx's social origins, it should be remembered that he was the son of a lawyer, a converted Jew from Trier, and Henrietta Pressburg. He was one of nine children. Marx's ancestors on both sides of the family had been rabbis, going back for generations. His paternal grandfather was the Rabbi of Trier, and a brother of his father's, his uncle Samuel, succeeded him. His mother's sister married a rich banker, the grandfather of the founder of the Dutch firm Philips. Marx married an aristocrat, Jenny Von Westphalen, and while he did live in poverty for part of his life, supported by Engels, his uncle Philips, and even by Lassalle, whom he hated, he nevertheless continued to lead a 'bourgeois' life. He despised Engels' mistress because their union had not been legitimized, and tried to conceal the evidence of his own extra-marital paternity. (He was the father of the child of Helene Demuth, the domestic servant in their house.)

The relation between Freud's Jewish origins and his discovery of psychoanalysis has often been described. The victim tries to discover the intentions of his oppressor and find his underlying motivation. The outcome is comprehension of the workings of the mind, its hidden detours. In fact, being persecuted also leads to self-observation which is undertaken to verify the truth or falsehood of the persecutor's accusations and compare the real self to the projections to which it is subjected. It was through his self-analysis that Freud discovered the laws of the unconscious. But Freud's Jewishness had also been brought to the fore by Marxists who suggest that he thus had a religious character, and that he was a product of the Vienna ghetto.

This may be the place to dispel a very popular myth: that of Vienna at the turn of the century as bourgeois and puritan on the one hand, whilst waltzing and eating *Sacher Torte* and *Strudel* on the other. In Freud's day, Vienna was the cultural cradle of Europe, even if he did not recognize its deeply innovative features. It was also the Vienna of Gustav Mahler, Schönberg and the dodecaphonists, of Husserl, Trotsky, who edited *Pravda* there during the seven years preceding World War I, of the Austro-Marxists, of Schnitzler, of Hofmannstahl, and later both Werfel and Rilke lived there or made frequent visits.

But what needs to be emphasized is the way in which

Freud lived his Jewishness. This cannot be separated from his relation to a lineage, to his father and the substitute figures of teacher and master. This factor must be very carefully evaluated; it is well known that there are many ways of living one's Jewishness, and that the kind of identification or counter-identification with the father which transmits, if not the religion, the cultural and moral tradition, is not to be overlooked.

We know that Freud, who was a firm atheist, was nevertheless strongly attached to Judaism as a cultural heritage, as a view of man and the relations between men. Because of the lack of mysticism in Judaism (in its rabbinical aspect at least), it possibly facilitates, perhaps to a greater extent than Christianity, the transition from religious faith to scientific thought. This, in fact, was Freud's own view and, in a letter to Abraham about Jung's introduction of religious thinking into psychoanalysis, he wrote: 'in the end things are easier for us other Jews, lacking as we do the mystical element'. But this absence of mysticism in Freud and in rabbinical Judaism must itself be put in the context of the subject's relation to God and to the father. This relation is different from that posited in Christianity, for in Judaism there is no miraculous substitution of the father by the son.

In this context Christianity and Judaism are to be understood as representing different 'models' of an oedipal solution. Christians and Jews do vary enormously individually; some go as far as to adopt the 'model' of the religion or culture to which they do not belong. Also, Christianity itself is a product of Judaism, which implies the possibility of a transformation of one model to another.

But for Freud the conflict between his relation to Judaism, on the one hand, and to his biological father on the other is a sign of his recognition of the place of the father-figure and of his place within a lineage, or ancestry. He affirmed his relation to Judaism in an address to the liberal Jewish Association, B'nai B'rith, in 1926 : 'The fact that you were Jews could only be agreeable to me; for I was myself a Jew, and it seemed not only unworthy but positively senseless to deny the fact'. And, trying to explain his attraction to Judaism, despite his firm atheism, he speaks of 'a clear consciousness of inner identity, the safe privacy of a common mental construction'. The sense of belonging could not be better expressed.

89

For Marx the relation was quite different: 'The tradition of all the past generations weighs like a nightmare upon the brain of the living,' he wrote. We also see Marx's antisemitism expressed in his writings on 'The Jewish Question', his reply to the book by Bruno Bauer; and also in his letters to Engels about Lassalle in which he refers to the latter as 'Itzig', a pejorative version of Isaac, a German equivalent of 'yid'. So that to stress Freud's Jewish identity, as do some Marxists, whilst overlooking the very significant relation that Marx had to his own Jewishness, is akin to the scotomization on the part of Catholic priests who 'forget' to tell the children to whom they teach the catechism that Christ was a Jew.

Now although Freud consciously maintained his sense of belonging throughout his life, it is possible to read *Moses and Monotheism* and find in it the return of the repressed antisemitism that every Jew carries within. It is the wish to unload the heavy burden of Jewishness. If Freud's study had been more carefully researched and if his correspondence did not reveal his almost compulsive relation to this work, it could probably be placed within a different context. His relation to his father – and from *The Interpretation of Dreams* we sense that it was close and warm – confirms a strong part of the Jewish tradition. To recall the famous incident narrated by Jakob as father and son were out walking and talking about 'his views on the things in the world we live in', a Gentile knocked Jakob's new fur hat into the gutter with a single swipe of his cane saying, 'Jew, get off the pavement!'

'And what did you do?' asked ten-year-old Sigmund.

'I went into the road and picked up my hat', was Jakob's quiet reply.

This story, which must have served to inform Sigmund of the meaning of being Jewish (that is, that he belonged to a heritage of those people who get their hats knocked off and who can only submit to the humiliation), was of great significance to Freud's psychic life. It reappears in a number of dreams and can be seen to contain a number of elements which would be likely to awaken unconscious anxieties and wishes: submission, castration, identification with the aggressor and with the victim.

But the representation of the paternal image can also be found in his father-substitutes. As Marthe Robert points out (Robert, 1964): 'Freud, like all strong personalities, had an inexhaustible capacity for admiration'. He did, in fact, admire a series of heroes often linked to Judaism: Hannibal the Semite, Cromwell and Napoleon, liberators of the Jews, and especially Moses. But he also admired his teachers, and in 'Some Reflections on Schoolboy Psychology', written for his school's centenary, he spoke of the interest that boys have in their teachers' personalities:

90

It is hard to decide whether what affected us more and was of greater importance to us was our concern with the sciences that we were taught or with the personalities of our teachers. It is true that this second concern was a perpetual undercurrent in all of us, and that in many of us the path to the sciences led only through our teachers . . . we studied their characters and on theirs we formed or misformed our own . . . We confronted them with the ambivalence that we had acquired in our own families and with its help we struggled with them as we had been in the habit of struggling with our fathers in the flesh. Unless we take into account our nurseries and our family homes, our behaviour to our schoolmasters would be not only incomprehensible but inexcusable (*S.E.*, *13*, 242, 244).

91

In *An Autobiographical Study* Freud describes his relation to his teachers in higher education. 'It was in Ernst Brücke's laboratory,' he writes, 'that I found men that I could respect and take as models.' He speaks of Brücke as 'my teacher, for whom I felt the highest possible esteem', and also of Meynert, 'by whose work and personality I had been greatly struck while I was still a student'. Freud went to Paris, drawn by Charcot's reputation, and offered to translate his book *Nouvelles Leçons*. Following his visit to Bernheim at Nancy, to study hypnosis, he translated two of his books, on suggestion and its therapeutic effects, into German.

The fact that Freud venerated heroes from history and his teachers is, no doubt, part of a Jewish heritage, but also reveals his own personality; for, if these figures represent the relation between the Jews and God the father, not every Jew conforms to this model, whereas many Christians do. It is likely, then, that what has been revealed as a Jewish heritage in Freud's relation to paternal figures is fundamentally linked with his personal relation, both resolved and unresolved, to his father. What remained unresolved is mostly to be found in his comparative silence on his relation to his mother, and his silence on maternal conflict in his theory in general, which influences his concepts of femininity.

It is often the case among Jewish men that the veneration of, or submission to, paternal figures is but the first phase of an ultimate identification with the father. The Jewish father is the patriarch in his home, and the young Sigmund became 'Freud', or, according to his own internal imagery, a Moses leading his people (disciples), to whom he gave the Law (psychoanalytic doctrine).

92

Freud's relationship to his lineage, and to his father, plays a part in his political scepticism. This relationship is characterized by the fact that ascendancy cannot be attained by a rejection or disowning of the lineage; and as such probably contributed to the discovery that psychic phenomena also exist in 'lineages' of affiliation. The infantile aetiology of mental illness, the determinism of mind, the ego as constituted by identification as well as by permanent and indestructible instincts, all imply that the present is only ever the product of the past, can only be understood as such, and that a total break, or *tabula rasa*, is impossible.

We often find that a dubious distinction is introduced as this point of the argument; the distinction between a political and an intellectual revolution. In our view, this is the product not only of erroneous thinking but also of a

deliberate desire to instil shame in every non-revolution-
ary, because on the intellectual level every mind is revolutionary which is able to cast a new light on the world and
so open up new perspectives on reality. This is true of all
scientific geniuses, many of whom lived and thought in
conservative ways outside the context of their work:
Lavoisier, Darwin, Pasteur, etc. People who put their
revolutionary spirit into political action are often incapable of genuinely creative work within the field of science.
('Politics precedes Science', *The Red Flag*, and 'The
Republic has no need of scientists' are two examples, the
latter was a statement used to justify the fact that Lavoisier was put to death during the French Revolution.)   *93*
We find that, in order to make discoveries, a mind that is
intellectually revolutionary needs to be able to acknowledge internal reality. The political revolutionary often
tries to deny internal reality by projecting the roots of his
conflicts on to society or external reality.

The psychoanalytic revolution has led to the question-
ing of all received ideas and prejudices; it has led to the
critical examination of all human culture, of political
systems and historical events in the light of the knowledge
of the unconscious. This is the most fundamental revolution. This is why all totalitarian regimes, whether of the
left or right, prohibit the dissemination and practice of
analysis. But in doing so they are less mistaken than those
intellectuals, and psychoanalysts, who claim that Freudian theory must only be applied to the study of mental
illness. For why should psychoanalysis be disruptive of
totalitarian regimes if not for the fact that it might, in
principle, give subjects a deeper understanding leading to
sharper criticism which is destructive of all ideology?

Those people who want to prevent psychoanalysis from
being practised outside the therapeutic context are very
close to those who want to prohibit it altogether; in fact,
they are exercising the 'religious prohibition on thinking'
that Freud described in 'A *Weltanschauung*'.

Freud seems only to have discussed the subject of revolution on one occasion, in the lecture cited above, when he
was answering criticisms which were already being made
of psychoanalysis as being a tool for 'adjustment':

> It has been said, and no doubt justly, that every educa-
> tion has a partisan aim, that it endeavours to bring the
> child into line with the established order of society,
> without considering how valuable or how stable that
> order may be in itself. If [it is argued] one is convinced
> of the defects in our present social arrangements, edu-
> cation within a psychoanalytic alignment cannot be
> justifiably put at their service as well: it must be given
> another and higher aim, liberated from the prevailing
> demands of society. In my opinion, however, this argu-
> ment is out of place here. Such a demand goes beyond
> the legitimate function of analysis. In the same way, it is
> not the business of a doctor who is called in to treat a
> case of pneumonia to concern himself with whether the
> patient is an honest man or a suicide or a criminal,
> whether he deserves to remain alive or whether one
> ought to wish him to. This other aim which it is desired
> to give to education will also be a partisan one, and it is
> not the affair of an analyst to decide between the par-
> ties. I am leaving entirely on one side the fact that
> psychoanalysis would be refused any influence on edu-
> cation if it admitted to intentions inconsistent with the

94

established social order. Psychoanalytic education will be taking an uninvited responsibility on itself if it proposes to mould its pupils into rebels. It will have played its part if it sends them away as healthy and efficient as possible. It itself contains enough revolutionary factors to ensure that no one educated by it will in later life take the side of reaction and suppression. It is not even my opinion that revolutionary children are desirable from any point of view (*S.E.*, *22*, 150–51).

CHAPTER IV

WILHELM REICH AND FREUDO-MARXISM
The Tragic Life of W.R.

WILHELM REICH would have liked children to be revolutionaries. He even wanted to bring about a revolution through children.

It is not the aim of this book to study all of Reich's writings; our intention is to show the profound incompatibility that exists between the Freudian project, as we have tried to show it, and that of Reich. This incompatibility existed from the very first. We can see it even in his apolitical writing such as *Character Analysis* (1927–1933)[4], where there are nevertheless some aspects of the work which are still valid in pure psychoanalysis.

First, however, it may be useful to give an outline of the tragedy of Wilhelm Reich's life. Although we have very little information about his childhood and adolescent years, there are a few comments in his biography by his last wife, Ilse Ollendorf Reich, which show that tragedy occurred very early in his life, and that this probably prefigured the more well-known tragedy of his later years.

Reich was born in 1897 in Dobrzcynica in Galicia, in

the region governed by the double monarchy. His Jewish family raised him non-religiously. There was a famous rabbi on the paternal side of the family. His mother came from a part of Austria which has since been reallocated to Rumania. His parents had a large agricultural estate in Bukovina. Ilse Ollendorf Reich writes:

> Many relatives told me that they were very well to do, highly regarded, rather snobbish, and thoroughly steeped in Germanic culture . . . The father was, by all accounts, a rather harsh man, acting as the lord and master to his employees and family alike, subject to violent rages, very much in love with his wife and very jealous of the attention she received from other men . . . Reich spoke very little of his relationship with his father. I got the impression that it was very ambivalent because he repeatedly made out that he was not his father's son, that his mother might have had an affair with one of the Ukrainian peasants – unlikely given the time and place – and he ultimately stretched this improbability to the point of claiming that he had been born of the union between his mother and a spaceman (Ollendorf Reich, 1969).

97

This is interesting if we remember that the 'family romance', which is so frequently found in paranoia, involves a repudiation of the father and a disavowal of affiliation;[5] Reich was manifestly paranoid at the point when he married Ilse Ollendorf, and she no doubt sensed this when she alludes to his ambivalence. We could also locate Reich's antisemitism on this axis of the disavowal of paternal lineage. In his interview with Kurt Eissler, *Reich*

Speaks of Freud (1952), Reich attributes Freud's short-comings to his Jewishness, at the same time as claiming that Freud was not a Jew on the level of 'character':

> He was not Jewish. He never felt Jewish. Similarly I never considered Anna Freud as Jewish. Neither of them had anything Jewish about them on the charac-terological, religious or national levels . . . Whilst Freud was a prisoner of Judaism I was not bound to it. I am much more in sympathy with the spiritual world of Christianity, with the Catholic mentality . . . Do you know what Christ knew? He knew the life force. I don't know if you understand. He had a humble understand-ing of the fields, of grass, of babies. That's what he knew. Freud didn't know.

There is no doubt that Reich's struggle with his father bears some relation to his struggle against 'patriarchal society'. But the existence of this relation is not, in itself, enough to invalidate his concepts on a deeper level.

Reich had two tutors, employed to prepare him for his entry into secondary school. One of them became his mother's lover. Reich reported this to his father, and his mother committed suicide. At this point Reich was four-teen years old. Ilse Ollendorf writes, 'To my mind, this event became one of the most crucial forces in his life . . . That Reich was unable to resolve this question [of guilt] may be one reason why he was never able to successfully finish his own analysis; there were several problems that he was never able to face'. The father, devastated by his wife's death, managed to catch pneumonia, developed tuberculosis, and died in 1914. Reich had a brother three years younger than himself. The two boys had always

been great rivals. The brother died in 1926. We can
assume that these events also had some bearing on
Reich's thought, on his psychosis, and on the general
direction of his life. (We hope that it will be acknowledged
that these events were, at least, more determining than
the fact that Reich belonged to the rural bourgeoisie.)
Apart from the fact that not every child would denounce
his mother to his father (this action was already symp-
tomatic), Reich's life developed in a way which is probably unique. He was, in effect, crucified on a cross, the
four arms of which could be thought of as National Socialism, the Communist Party, the International Psychoanalytic Association, and the American Administration. At
the close of his life, he identified strongly with Christ
(Reich, 1953, 48). This quadruple anathema was sufficient cause for the New Left to deify him, and there were
also his writings, which encapsulate the wishes and ideas
of a lot of contemporary politics.

Typically, when Roger Crémant had the nerve to satir-
ize some of Reich's politico-sexual ideas in *Le Nouvel Obser-
vateur*, the editors received an avalanche of protest from
readers (some of whom, to our knowledge, were neither
Marxists nor Freudians, nor Freudo-Marxists). Roger
Crémant did not publish again in that magazine. Is it
mere coincidence?

Reich came across psychoanalysis in the course of his
medical studies thanks to Paul Federn, who used to invite
the impecunious student to dinner. As Reich was very
poor during this period the occasions provided an opportunity to eat as well as to talk. It is significant that Federn
was later to become Reich's main 'persecutor' from the
psychoanalytic world. The persecutor, in a paranoid

delusion, is always a former libidinal object; Paul Federn
was the author of major works on *Ego Psychology and the
Psychoses* (1952), in which he discusses the way that the
body is experienced in various psychotic states and in the
splitting of the libido into objectal and narcissistic modes.
(His conclusions were often different from those of Freud.
He became President of the Vienna Psychoanalytic
Society.)

> But then Federn came along. He was a Modju. Federn
> was a psychoanalytic Modju. (Modju was derived from
> Mocenigo . . . who delivered Giordano Bruno, a very
> great scientist, to the Inquisition in the sixteenth cen-
> tury . . . that's MO-cenigo. And Dju is Djugashvilli,
> that's Stalin, Josef, Vissarionovich Djugashvilli. So I
> put it together to make 'Modju'. Modju is a synonym
> for the emotional plague or pestilent character who uses
> underhand slander and defamation in his fight against
> life and truth.) There is evidence that in 1924 this man
> began to 'dig' at Freud against me. I didn't know it
> then. Freud didn't know it. It became clear later on. He
> was jealous of my success. (Reich, 1952, 18, 116).

Even if Federn really had intervened against W.R. the
kind of motivations that Reich ascribes to him are nonetheless significant. He 'dug at' Freud against him; he was
'jealous' of his success. The same accusation of jealousy,
this time straightforwardly sexual, is repeated with
Sándor Radó, Reich's second analyst (the first was
Sadger): 'Emmy, Radó's wife, and I had very strong
genital contact with each other. Never anything like full
embrace happened between us but we danced a lot
together and we had very strong contact. And Radó was

jealous . . . He was the one who started that rumour in 1934. He began the rumour that I was schizophrenic' (1952, 112). It is, however, extremely unlikely that there is any truth in the claim of such a 'rumour' being started by any analyst of Reich's as to his being schizophrenic, if only because he was obviously not schizophrenic but did, in fact, suffer from paranoia. He showed no signs of the dissociation which characterizes schizophrenia, and his work has all the signs of systematic coherence even in its most delirious moments. As for jealousy, Reich, in his book *The Invasion of Compulsory Sex Morality*, attributes this emotion to the sense of possession, which he claims is a relatively recent human acquisition, the effect of legal regulation. Towards the end of his life Reich was susceptible to violent fits of jealousy.

On the subject of Elsa Lindenberg, Reich's companion after his first divorce, Ilse Ollendorf notes:

> Always in times of stress, one of Reich's very human failings came to the foreground, and that was his violent jealousy. He would always emphatically deny that he was jealous, but there is no getting away from the fact that he would accuse his wife of infidelity with any man who came to his mind as a possible rival, whether colleague, friend, local shopkeeper, or casual acquaintance (Ollendorf Reich, 45).

Here we can recall his father's jealousy too.

In the course of his medical studies Reich married Annie Pink with whom he had two children. They separated in 1933. Annie Reich, who died in 1971, was a highly respected figure in psychoanalysis. Her contributions to the problem of early identification, the formation of the female superego, and the ego ideal, are in no way 'Reichian'.

Reich joined the Vienna Psychoanalytic Society in 1919. His first paper was entitled 'Libidinal Conflicts and Delusions in Ibsen's *Peer Gynt*'. It is clear that, from the start, his interest was in the theory of the libido. 'His main concept always from the very beginning was the energy concept', writes Ilse Ollendorf. In 1923 he published an article in the Review of Sexology, *Zeitschrift für Sexual-wissenschaft*, concerning 'The Energy of the Drives'. In the same year he published his own article 'On Genitality'. In 1922 Freud had founded the Psychoanalytic Polyclinic in Vienna, and Reich became its first assistant until 1928, and then the assistant director until he left Vienna in 1930. 'He began, at that time, in 1924, his studies into the social causation of mental illness' (Ollendorf Reich,10). From 1924 to 1930 he led the Psychoanalytic Technique Seminar. His idea of a 'muscle armour' made its appearance in 1928 in an article 'On Character Analysis'. It was early in 1927 that the conflict between Freud and Reich surfaced. According to Annie Reich, it was less to do with any disagreement about the politics of psycho-analysis than with the fact that Freud refused to analyse him. This was because of the rule made by the founder of psychoanalysis that he would not treat members of the Vienna circle. While this was going on Reich developed tuberculosis and left for Davos. (His father and brother both died of T.B.) There he finished the first version of *The Function of the Orgasm* (1927). A second version appeared in 1942, containing additions about the 'discov-ery' of orgone.

As early as 1927 (actually as far back as 1923 in his

102

article 'On Genitality') Reich claimed that orgastic incapacity is not the result of neurosis, but is its cause. This
concept, in fact, sums up his entire psychoanalytic, and
even political, theory. He joined the Communist Party in
1928 (and later denied having been an active member: 'I
was never a political Communist. I would like to have that
fully on record. Never. Oh yes, I worked in the organization, I worked with them' (Reich, 1952, 114)). He set up
centres for information on sexual health in early 1929. In
the same year he published *Dialectical Materialism and
Psychoanalysis* in Moscow, the first truly Freudo-Marxist
text. In 1930 he left Vienna for Berlin, where Sándor
Radó, with whom he was to begin his second analysis, was   *103*
living. In 1931 he founded SEXPOL (SExual POLitik).
SEXPOL organized meetings, consultations and lectures
on the liberalization of abortion laws, the sexual education of children, contraception, marriage and divorce and
legal reform, as well as on the 'sexual misery' of young
people and on housing, etc. In September 1929 Reich had
visited Moscow and had seen Vera Schmidt's 'Kindergar-
tens'. In Germany SEXPOL had between twenty- and
forty-thousand members. Most of its pamphlets were
written by Reich, including *The Sexual Struggle of Youth*. *The
Invasion of Compulsory Sex Morality* appeared in 1932, a book
responding to Malinowski's *The Sexual Life of Savages*.
Reich was particularly taken with Malinowski's ideas on
the transition from matriarchy to patriarchy and the connections between patriarchy, repression and totalitarian-
ism. At this point Reich was still a member of the
International Psychoanalytic Association, by virtue of his
membership of the Berlin Society. In this book he comes
across as profoundly dissident, although less so through

his political theory than through his conception of the Oedipus complex. In fact, the two levels are closely linked, as his political theories determine his conception of the Oedipus complex, and *vice-versa*.

When Reich left for Berlin, Annie Reich and their two daughters followed him:

> Reich's identification with the proletarian movement was so great at that time that he put before his wife the alternative of either placing the children in a Communist children's centre or agreeing to a separation. Annie consented to the children being sent to the home, although she feels today that this was a great mistake on her part. The children recall the home as a very unhappy experience (Ollendorf Reich, 23).

104

Contrary to his plans, *Character Analysis* was not published by the '*Internationaler Psychoanalytischer Verlag*', but by the '*Sexpol Verlag*' in 1933.

While the conflict between Reich and the psychoanalytic movement was coming to a head, the German Communist Party deemed his ideas to be 'deviationist' with regard to orthodox Marxism, and they criticized his work with young people. According to the Party, the emphasis he placed on sexuality diverted young people from revolutionary activity rather than propelling them towards it. He was expelled from the Party in 1933.

> Only absolutes were possible for Reich. Something was either black or white; you were for him or against him; never a compromise, never a shade of grey permissible . . . It was this inflexible attitude of his, more than

anything else, that again and again lost him friends and co-workers (24).

(This kind of rigidity is characteristic of the paranoiac's personality.)

Hitler's rise to power led to the separation between Reich and his first wife; they were now estranged politically, theoretically, over the clinical practice of psychoanalysis and over the education of their children. On top of all this, Reich had started a relationship with Elsa Lindenberg, the dancer mentioned above, whom he met at a May Day demonstration in 1932.

Reich wanted to take refuge in Denmark, to practise there as a training analyst (that is, analysing future analysts) and as a teaching analyst. After much deliberation, the Psychoanalytic Association did not grant him the status of training analyst in Denmark. In August 1933, Reich published *The Mass Psychology of Fascism*,[6] in Denmark, where Elsa Lindenberg had come to join him. When his visitor's visa was not renewed after a six-month stay, Reich went to London. There he found analysts were unreceptive to his ideas, especially those expressed in *The Invasion of Compulsory Sex Morality*, as this book and Malinowski's had been subject to negative criticism from British colleagues. He finally settled in Malmö, Sweden, maintaining contact with those Danish analysts who shared his political beliefs, working with sex education, family planning, abortion, etc. In June 1934 the Swedish authorities withdrew his visitor's permit. It was the Norwegian analysts that Reich felt especially close to, and one in particular, Ola Raknes, followed him through his 'dis-

covery' of orgone and all the more bizarre ideas that
followed.

In 1933, Reich was repeatedly asked to resign from the
International Psychoanalytic Association. He refused.
The day before the Lucerne Congress (1934) he was told
that he would no longer be listed among the members, but
that this fact should not be a personal hindrance to him,
given his 'reputation'. 'It must be admitted that his work
had taken a very personal direction which distanced him
from the parent organization', says Ilse Ollendorf Reich.
In the 1942 edition of *The Function of the Orgasm* Reich
himself states that: 'To understand my later difficulties
with Freud it must be noted that there were visible divergences from the first stages of my work'.

106

One episode in the 'difficulties' with Freud and Freudian psychoanalysis is noteworthy. It was to do with
Reich's description of the 'Masochistic Character', which
includes an argument refuting the existence of the death
instinct. 'Suffering has its origin in the outside world, in
repressive society', the death instinct does not exist. However, even if there is no death instinct this does not mean
that aggression and suffering are only responses to
'repression' or frustration of external origin. Clearly,
Reich could not accept the idea of a death instinct because
to do so would invalidate many of his criticisms of society.[7]
Freud himself was aware of the 'metaphysical' nature of
his new instinctual dualism (Eros/Thanatos), and introduced it as part of a highly speculative process, but there
is also something very ambiguous in Reich's need to
reduce all human suffering to a 'conflict between the
instincts and the outside world'. This reduction is followed by a rationalization, which is facilitated by Reich's

adherence to Marxism. Reich's ambiguity seems to have been mirrored in Freud's reaction to this article. According to Freud, the 'Masochistic Character' (1933) was to have been published with a note mentioning Reich's membership of the Communist Party. Reich refused. In the end it was decided that the article would be followed by a comment from Siegfried Bernfeld, a leftist analyst, discussing Reich's position and that of the Marxists *vis-à-vis* Freudianism, giving Reich the right to reply. It seems that Freud found himself in a very uncomfortable position, as he had never considered his own concept of the death instinct as being necessarily part of the metapsychology (unlike the Oedipus complex, infantile sexuality, transference, repression and resistance). He completely accepted the fact that many analysts (Ernest Jones included) rejected the concept of the death instinct. So Freud's reaction to this article was not motivated by Reich's refutation of the death instinct; it was probably a response to the entire subtext of Reich's conflicts with him, to which Freud sought to ascribe a political basis. This, in our view, was quite wrong of him and was a collusion with the manifest content of Reich's theories, instead of seeing them as the 'secondary elaboration', the latent content of which would not be hard to find. Secondary elaboration, or secondary revision, is the 'rearrangement of a dream so as to present it in the form of a relatively consistent and comprehensible scenario' – (Laplanche & Pontalis, 1973). The authors rightly cite a passage from *Totem and Taboo* where Freud likens secondary elaboration to the formation of certain systems of thought.

     In October 1934, Reich settled in Oslo. The Institute of

Psychology at Oslo University put at his disposal everything he needed to start his long-awaited 'experiments on
the bioelectric nature of sexuality and anxiety' (Ollendorf
Reich, 33). The era of 'experimentation' and 'scientific
discoveries' had begun, and was to end only with Reich's
death.

J.M. Palmier writes:

Everything written by Reich on politics from this time
on is without interest and is terribly sad when compared with his earlier works. It seems that the double
exclusion, from the German C.P. and from the International Psychoanalytic Association from which he was
soon to be debarred, triggered off delusions of persecution . . . Reich added nothing to what he had already
said, he repeated it, shouted it even, but each time with
less depth and with greater mysticism, if we can use this
term to describe the biological delusions which slowly
took over his thought.

It is no betrayal of Reich to recognise reality: what
comparison can there be between his first works written
in Vienna and Berlin, and the hotchpotch of fake
experiments, delusional ideas, insults, the laughable
medley of his later writings, published when he was still
in Norway or after his exile to the United States
(Palmier, 148).

It is no betrayal of the truth to draw such comparisons
between the early and later works. We shall do so, spurred
on by the fact that there are two versions of *The Functions of
the Orgasm* (one from 1927, the other from 1942) of which it
is now being claimed that the second is delusional but not

the first. In fact, the first already contained the kernel of the second.

In *The Triumph of the Therapeutic* (1966) Philip Rieff describes his study of Reich as an attempt to examine the 'continuum between the brilliance and the absurdities of Reich's work'. The author notes, quite rightly in our opinion, that '*Character Analysis* has been greatly overrated in order that Reich's later works may be more stringently criticized'; adding that 'these critiques have recourse to that dubious process which consists of separating a writer's early works from the later ones in order to criticize one or other' resulting in 'the refusal to confront the significant correlation between science and fantasy in Reich's mind' (170).

109

If Reich's psychosis was only evident by 1934, it had nevertheless been latent for a long time. The reason it was not evident to everyone was that, as in many cases of paranoia, the coherent and systematic appearance of ideas is a symptom which allows the subject to function in an apparently normal way. The internal necessity that forces paranoiacs to persuade others as to the reality of their system of belief results in their 'recruiting' converts. These disciples will tend to be seduced by the paranoiac's ideas in so far as these deny reality and mobilize Illusion; an illusion which will be backed by manic rationalization. Right up until the end Reich had many disciples, including medical doctors and scientists. In any case, it is not possible for a psychiatrist, still less a psychoanalyst, to believe that paranoia might irrupt in a subject who had not, at some previous time, shown a character with traits of a latent paranoia, with those fixations which are characteristic of this illness, such as homosexuality and narcissism. Of course, 'humiliations and social rejections' play a part in triggering off a delusion. Freud linked these injuries to a disappointment in the sphere of sublimated homosexuality – that is, in the esteem or regard of the subject's peers – which leads to a resexualization of passive homosexuality. This becomes the source of a particularly acute conflict in the latent paranoiac: 'The irruption of the return of the repressed . . . takes its start from the point of fixation, and it implies a regression of the libidinal development to that point' (1911, *S.E.*, *12*, 68).

With his expulsion from the Communist Party and from the International Psychoanalytic Association, Reich suffered a blow to his narcissism that might have had the capacity to precipitate a psychotic process. But it should be understood that the difference between the period of the 'discoveries' and the earlier period is far from clear-cut. Reich had been planning, for a long time, to conduct experiments, and colleagues had, for a long time, thought him ill. In *Civilization and its Discontents*, which Reich claimed was written as a response to his own theories, Freud wrote:

110

> Another procedure operates more energetically and more thoroughly. It regards reality as the sole enemy and as the source of all suffering, with which it is impossible to live, so that one must break off all relations with it if one is to be in any way happy. The hermit turns his back on the world and will have no truck with it. But one can do more than that; one can try to recreate the world, to build up in its stead another world in which its most unbearable features are eliminated and replaced by others that are in conformity with

one's own wishes. But whoever, in desperate defiance, sets out upon this path to happiness will as a rule attain nothing. Reality is too strong for him. He becomes a madman, who for the most part finds no one to help him in carrying though his delusion. [Freud is wrong here; paranoiacs are often leaders.] It is asserted, however, that each one of us behaves in some respect like a paranoiac, corrects some aspect of the world which is unbearable to him by the construction of a wish and introduces this delusion into reality (*S.E.*, *21*, 81).

To recapitulate, then, Reich's exclusion from the International Psychoanalytic Association was the result of the undeniable schism, which existed from the outset, between Freudian theory and his own, these theories differing over issues more fundamental than the question of the death drive. To repeat, it seems wrong to us, and superficial, to attribute the divergences between Reich and Freud to political issues. There was a basic and essential theoretical divergence that led Reich to Freudo-Marxism. There had always been militant socialists and even ultraleftists among analysts, even in Freud's time (Fenichel, Bernfeld, Ferenczi, Radó, etc.).

Alongside his laboratory research and his lectures, Reich wrote a great number of articles on political psychology and sexual economy between 1934 and 1939. In 1936 he founded the Institute of Research into the Biology of Sexual Economy, a huge building comprising three lecture theatres, labs and a publication committee. He then encountered problems with his collaborators, as Ilse Ollendorf remembers:

Some young socialists insisted on a political way of

running the publishing house with equal rights for everybody. When Reich, in his rather forceful way, insisted on his rights, he was called a dictator (Ollendorf Reich, 36).

Here we can see a comparison with the way in which Reich's father treated his subordinates. The paranoiac, who is afraid of his passive homosexuality, always tries to impose himself, which forces him to become a leader.

During the same period Reich gave up psychoanalysis altogether and created 'Vegetotherapy', which, according to Ilse Ollendorf, 'did away with the psychoanalytic taboo of never touching a patient', the therapist provoking 'a violent muscular spasm'. Those who have seen the film *W.R., Mysteries of the Organism* will have some idea of the type of therapy involved. A. S. Neill, the author of *The Free Child* (1913) and founder of Summerhill Free School, came to Reich to be initiated into his technique and remained a friend throughout his life.

Then, in 1937, Reich discovered 'bions', bioelectrical units of life energy. In 1938 he wrote a book about his discovery (*Die Bione*) and applied himself to the 'biopathy' of cancer. There is something tragic about this manic research when one considers that it was linked with a desire to cure Freud; and so was also linked to his guilt and to his very ambivalent relation to the founder of psychoanalysis. (He always kept, in pride of place, an autographed photo of Freud, and in 1936 he produced a booklet entitled *Our Wishes to Freud* as a tribute to Freud's eightieth birthday.) The relation between this research and Freud's cancer is explicit in the following passage from the interview *Reich Speaks of Freud*: 'But to come back

112

to Freud. He was very beautiful at that Congress (Berlin 1923), as he always was when he spoke. Then it hit him just here in the mouth. And that is where my interest in cancer began. I began cancer studies in 1926–1927'. This was to lead to the publication of *The Cancer Biopathy* (1948), the second volume of *The Discovery of the Orgone*.

Reading this book is heartbreaking. The description of fatally ill people visiting Reich, when medicine could offer them no hope, like pilgrims going to Lourdes; the minutiae of haematological observations of 'biophysical orgone' in cultures, the biological resistance tests including the detection of 'blue bions', followed by descriptions of a cure through 'orgone radiation'; and finally the   *113* ascription of the illness to highly speculative aetiological factors reduced to 'stasis neurosis' (due to the absence of orgasmic discharge) are as tragic as his statements like 'we shall soon come to see that cancerous metastases will develop in those organs which play a leading role in the muscle armour that represses sexual excitation'. Reich discovered a 'blue orgonic zone', along with the 'blue bions' mentioned above, and was later to develop this aspect of his discovery:

> Blue is the specific colour of orgone energy within and without the organism . . . protoplasm of any kind, in every cell or bacterium is blue . . . Thunderclouds are deeply blue, due to high orgone charges contained in the suspended masses of water . . . Water in deep lakes and in the ocean is blue. The luminating tail ends of glow-worms are blue, as St Elmo's fire and the *aurora borealis* ('The Orgone Energy Accumulator – Its Scientific and Medical Use', 1952, 15).

We are now in the midst of a mystical, delusional system which attempts to prove the omnipotence of the psyche. The body is seen as potentially eternal. Only the psyche makes it vulnerable, only the psyche can cure – or more particularly, only orgone, the life energy. We will now try to unearth the significance or meaning of this fantasy.

Many analysts, in the course of their training, are tempted to try to find psychogenetic causes for every organic illness, and even to deny physical illness itself. 'It's psychic', they say. This tendency is an attempt to deny illness, to deny castration. In such cases, the desire to become an analyst is the desire to take unto oneself (in fantasy) the mysterious power of the unconscious, to tame or control it, and so become more powerful than death. When this desire is implicated in the choice of psycho-analysis as a 'profession' it must be analysed in the candidate. A person struggling with an overwhelming castration anxiety (which is linked to passive homosexual wishes) can try to resolve this by developing a delusional belief in his own omnipotence. Seeing himself as gifted with a supernatural power, or inventing a particular therapeutic method thanks to the 'discovery' of a natural force which he can use (orgone, for example), such a person gives himself proof of his own invulnerability. He is even able, he thinks, to help others and to conquer illness, ageing, decay and death. Because of this it is not unusual to find many paranoiacs among healers, although it would be incorrect to call them charlatans as their aim is not to deceive others but to deceive themselves. (Ilse Ollendorf tells us that 'Dr Ola Raknes once said that Reich may have needed to assert himself continuously because often he may have been unsure of his own

114

theories' (40).) A psychosomatic theory of cancer is not impossible, but it has yet to be formulated. And the aetiology of the localization of cancerous tumours assimilated to specific points of a character armour makes Reich's project particularly absurd. In *The Function of the Orgasm* (1942) Reich contends that all malignant tumours are the result of undischarged sexual energy. In fact Reich reduces all mental and physical illness to a single cause: sexual stasis. The fact that there were intelligent people who believed in his discoveries only serves to show the vulnerability of the human mind, which is always ready to believe in anything that answers to certain wishes, is always susceptible to Illusion.

115

In Norway, Reich's book on bions started a media campaign which, according to Ilse Ollendorf, turned abusive. Reich was called 'the charlatan of psychoanalysis', a 'Jewish pornographer', and 'Reich/God created Life'. The last of these accusations contains some truth as a comment on Reich's state of mind; his 'discovery' of orgone and bions is quite simply a variant of the theory of spontaneous generation. Like God, Reich created life *ex nihilo*: 'When I demonstrate, for example, that completely sterilized substances can produce life, people reply that the experiment dish was dirty, or that if there seems to be life it is only due to the effect of Brownian movement.' On this score the back-cover of *Character Analysis* gives cause for concern. The English language edition of the book has a third section which is called 'From Psychoanalysis to the Biophysics of Orgone', and so includes writings which date from the period when Reich's madness was manifest (an illness which even the most fervent of Reichians acknowledge); and the back-cover carries the suggestion that the orgone theory has been accepted as scientific truth. It states:

> It presents revolutionary insights into one of the hardest problems of psychiatry, schizophrenia, in the dramatic and moving case history of the first schizophrenic ever to be treated with orgone therapy . . . It takes character analysis out of the realm of psychology and puts it on the firm basis of natural science, in the form of orgone biophysics.

One can only hope that this statement is a product of the Wilhelm Reich Infant Trust Fund, which is one of the groups dedicated to defending and promoting his works, especially his later ones.

116

Reich's psychosis surfaced with increasing violence; he tended to have explosive outbursts of anger and became 'suspicious and wary . . . He was afraid that people might steal some of his discoveries – a fear that stayed with him until the end of his life' (Ollendorf Reich, 46). Ilse Ollendorf writes of the way in which Reich, who had always insisted (quite rightly) on the importance of negative transference, could not bear it in his own patients. One of them told how Reich's reaction to him was 'slapping me down to such an extent that it took years to recover from it' (47). We are told, in *The Function of the Orgasm* (253), that during the period of his study on the masochistic character he once beat a patient, in order to find out whether he was really looking for pain.

After increasingly frequent episodes of conflict with his co-workers, Reich set out for New York on 19 August 1939. It was in the United States that he built the first 'orgone accumulator'. He sought out Einstein, who received him amicably and listened for several hours as he told of his 'discoveries'. Einstein took a week to consider the matter, and then wrote Reich a polite letter in which he explained the experimental faults and the natural phenomena which could account for the conclusions drawn by Reich. Reich then became very hostile towards Einstein, whom he henceforth considered to be part of a Communist conspiracy directed against his work. (Reich wrote a pamphlet about this, called 'The Einstein Affair'.) Reich next set up the 'Cancer Research Laboratory', then the 'Orgone and Cancer Research Laboratories', and finally the 'Orgone Institute Research Laboratories Inc.'. He taught with a doctor called Wolfe and, according to Ilse Ollendorf, 'he complained that orgonotherapy was becoming an excellent way to make a lot of money'.

117

In the summer of 1942, Reich bought a large plot of land in Maine, on which he built, in the years that followed, laboratories, lecture theatres, an observatory and housing for the inhabitants of what he called 'Organon', a sort of ideal city where he hoped to set up 'the democracy of work'. He had met Ilse Ollendorf in 1939 and they had a son in 1944. Ilse Ollendorf recalls how 'Reich was always very afraid of being caught in the middle of outbursts of natural forces beyond his control, such as thunderstorms, gales or fires'. Here again, the best way to avoid fear in the face of 'outbursts of natural forces', and everything they might symbolize, is to try to harness them, to control them. This led to 'rain-making' with the help of 'cloudbusters' which also helped to get rid of deadly orgone or DOR, DOR being the result of 'the invasion into space of parasites infesting the earth'. Ilse Ollendorf compares this to air pollution. In fact, this emphasis on the fear of pollution tends to activate the core of paranoia that each of us carries within us, to different degrees, and does so whatever the reality of the external situation may be. Ilse Ollendorf considered the cloudbusters or DORbusters to be a very good thing, with the capacity to combat air pollution.

After receiving authorization from the Ministry of Wartime Production, orgone energy accumulators (for which steel was required) were manufactured. Next was the production of accumulators that could extract DOR from the body, which were used by doctors. 'In the United States, as elsewhere, Reich's work continued to awaken a growing interest. A voluminous correspondence continued between foreign scientists and many other people who were curious about his writings, study groups regularly sent reports describing experimental work conducted in England, Denmark, Switzerland and Italy.' Reich came to measure orgone energy with a Geiger counter. At the same time, the mystical side of the whole process was accentuated: orgonic energy is cosmic energy which can be 'traced back to God . . . God was in us and around us like orgonic energy'. Reich, in fact, continually oscillated between persecution and mysticism, and the latter clearly protected him from the former. Ilse Ollendorf tells how Reich always refused to treat homosexuals and, when a colleague referred a very worthy professional man to him for treatment, he not only refused to accept him but said: 'I don't want to deal with such filth'. He also refuted sexology, claiming that 'sexology deals with Indian phalli, condoms and homosexual perversions (83)'. Ilse Ollendorf traces this attitude of his back to unresolved personal conflicts. According to the Freudian

118

theory of paranoia, this psychosis has its roots in the fear of passive homosexual wishes.

The ORANUR experiment was intended to exorcize the nuclear threat. In fact, using radioactivity as it did, it made everyone who participated in it ill, including Ilse Ollendorf and their son Peter. It was after this experiment that Reich began to plan his book, *The Murder of Christ.* At the same time, he started to believe in spacecraft. Ilse Ollendorf describes the escalation of his fantasies of being persecuted throughout this time, which also had the effect of making him a persecutor:

> Reich was worried at that time that I would become an enemy and slander him. Therefore he used exactly the same stratagems to protect himself that he had furiously attacked in others, especially the Stalinists. He demanded again and again that I write 'confessions' about my feelings of fear of the work, occasional feelings of fear and hate about him, and he took these 'confessions' and locked them away . . . I had to give him once a statement about all the things he had given me during the years of our marriage, including such items as birthday and Christmas gifts, and payments of hospital bills during my confinement and operation (113).

119

Reich kept the American Government informed of his experiments, which he considered to be of great importance for the welfare of mankind in general and of the United States in particular. In a sad attempt to split off the object of danger, he claimed that he was protected from his enemy the 'Red Fascists' by the Air Force and the President. He thought that extra-terrestrials were running spacecraft on orgonic energy and that DOR consis-

ted of the exhaust fumes from their machines. Earth was
being submitted to attacks from space, and when we recall
that Reich claimed to be the son of a spaceman, it is not
hard to see the underlying fantasy of a primal scene on a
cosmic scale. Reich continued his experiments with 'rain-
making' and the cloudbuster became a spacegun.

The American Medical Association and the American
Psychiatric Association began to stir. Warning letters
were sent to a number of orgonotherapists in early 1953.
The following February, the Food and Drug Administration banned the sale of orgone accumulators. 'Reich', says
Ilse Ollendorf, 'made me the butt of his wrath against the
outside world. I was a murderer . . . I belonged with all
those who murder life wherever it tries to function in a
healthy way. I understood that I only represented the
outside world that he detested so' (120). Reich turned to
drink. In November 1954 Ilse Ollendorf left him. According to Reich, the FDA was controlled by the Communists.
He tried to annul the court order prohibiting the sale of
orgone accumulators. He argued that no court of law was
entitled to pass judgment on scientific discoveries. The
FDA led an inquiry into the Orgone Institute's publications on the cancer cases treated with orgonotherapy
and pronounced them 'medical publicity'. This accusation was extended to all the books published by the
Orgone Institute Press, including those that had nothing
to do with the 'discovery' of orgone, merely because they
contained the words 'cancer' or 'blood'.

When Ilse Ollendorf left him, Reich found another
partner, Grethe Hoff, one of his past students, and soon
began to torture her with his jealousy. He also made her
write confessions.

120

He decked out Organon, as if for an official visit; he was waiting for his 'protector', the President of the United States, Eisenhower, to come and visit him. He re-read Rousseau and the New Testament. It must be said that if some of Reich's friends and collaborators abandoned him at this point, others remained loyal to him to the end. This was not only to give support to somebody who was deeply unhappy, but also because they actually shared his beliefs, including his conviction that the earth was being attacked by spacemen.

In late 1955, he found himself a new companion, one of his admirers, a beautiful young biologist, Aurora Karrer. Meanwhile, the FDA continued to gather evidence against Reich, who considered it not only a Communist conspiracy but 'Evil in general'. He refused legal help. He never spoke at the hearings, claiming that he was bound to silence by a state secret. When the sale of orgone accumulators was banned he sent a long letter to the court, refusing to conform to legal procedures. Thus, the FDA obtained, by default, an order for the destruction of accumulators and of all the publications of the Orgone Institute Press which might be considered to be 'propaganda' or 'medical publicity'. In October of the same year, the Orgone Institute Press informed the Legal Department that it would continue its scientific work and would continue to distribute its publications. Without going into the fine details of the ensuing events, including Organon's armed reception of the FDA officials, it is not hard to sense the unusual nature of this conflict. On the one side was the American administration and the judiciary and, on the other, a man who signed every document EPPO, the Emotional Plague Prevention Office (Reich had a tendency to call everything he considered as an attack on life by the name of Emotional Plague).

Ilse Ollendorf , who was cited as a witness, was asked by the judge whether she thought that Reich should be asked to undergo a psychiatric examination, which might have proved a way out of the legal problem. Ilse Ollendorf refused to judge. Reich was finally sentenced to two years' imprisonment. The publications of the Orgone Institute Press were destroyed. The over-zealous officials destroyed not only those books published by the Press, but Reich's entire library. At the penitentiary the psychiatric experts diagnosed a condition of paranoia, but decided not to make a statement of the diagnosis. Ilse Ollendorf says: 'They did not feel that much could be gained by reopening the entire case for reasons of legal insanity, and they felt a man of Reich's standing should not be made to suffer from the label of legal insanity. I think this latter decision was an honourable one' (154). Reich still believed that he was being protected by the Air Force each time a plane flew over the penitentiary. At the same time, he believed he was being poisoned by a lotion which had been prescribed for his eczema, from which he had always suffered and which had become particularly acute during the last years. He died of a heart attack on 3 November 1957.

The funeral was very much an extension of Reich's tragic life: 'There was already before the funeral a takeover by a number of "pure Reichians" who wanted to exclude others from the funeral' (159). Ilse Ollendorf remembers that the ceremony bordered on mass hysteria. So began the posthumous career of Wilhelm Reich. It is not over yet.

If we have dwelt at length on the sad story of the life of the

author of *The Sexual Revolution*, and on describing his paranoia, it is because we feel that this left its mark on his
entire work. Of course, the fact that an idea is expressed
by someone with a mental illness does not necessarily
make it wrong (nor does it necessarily make it right).
Sometimes certain character structures can lend a special
sensitivity towards aspects of reality, if not the real world
in its entirety, and this can help to uncover aspects of that
reality that may usually be overlooked. In Reich's case,
quite apart from the truth or otherwise of his theories, we
can see the effects of his psychosis in their distance from
Freudianism. This might be unimportant were it not for
the fact that Reich's paranoia, like Rousseau's, can come
to superimpose itself on our own; for in every one of us
there is a core of paranoia which can be activated to
varying extents. And we are often all too willing to accept,
with some relief, those systems of thought which may
shore up the defences which are characteristic of this
illness.

CHAPTER V

REICH'S WORK AS DISAVOWAL OF INFANTILE SEXUALITY

WE WILL CONSIDER Reich's work, and its impact, as these are indicative of the phenomenon of paranoia. But before doing so, we will examine the way in which his work acts to cover up the Freudian scandal – the discovery of infantile sexuality.[8]

It may seem paradoxical, at first sight, to claim that the work of an author who campaigned for *The Sexual Struggle of Youth* (1932) (in the 1949 preface to the fourth edition of *The Sexual Revolution* he recalls that, having defended 'the rights of children and adolescents to natural love', he also rebelled against 'pulpiteers of all faiths, socialists, Communists, psychologists, doctors, psychoanalysts', enemies of 'the genital games of all children' who were horrified at 'the single thought that young people can satisfy their sexual needs though natural embraces') was in fact motivated by a deep and absolute need to reject infantile sexuality. Moreover, in 1927, Reich published a paper in the *Zeitschrift für psychoanalytische Pädagogik*, in which he recommends nudity 'in games, bathing, between parents and children, teachers and pupils, and the satisfaction of the child's sexual curiosity'. He states that:

> The child's request to witness sexual relations could be refused but this would already constitute a restriction of an accepting attitude towards sexuality . . . We should boldly acknowledge that our refusal to let the child be present during the sexual act is not the result of considering the interests of the child but of our wish not to be disturbed in our pleasure.

This does, admittedly, make our thesis appear somewhat extreme, since Reich seems to hold pedagogic views that are fully cognizant of infantile sexual desire. (We will return later to question the kind of thinking which underlies 'liberal' or 'permissive' educational practice.) We shall, nevertheless, examine the issue more closely.

There is no doubt that the theory of the libido, or sexual energy, was central to Reich's interests from the outset. It is a concept borrowed from Freud, who refers to it in his correspondence with Fliess as early as 1893, and again in his paper 'On the Grounds for Detaching a Particular Syndrome from Neurasthenia under the Description "Anxiety Neurosis"' (1894, *S.E.*, *3*, 87–115). The paper on 'Sexuality in the Aetiology of the Neuroses' (1898), in which Freud introduces the concept of 'actual neurosis', is also founded on the concept of the libido. Reich was to take up this concept of 'actual neurosis' and to use it almost exclusively. *Three Essays on the Theory of Sexuality* (1905) develops the theory of the libido. The great steps forward in the Freudian theory of the instincts are very clearly linked to the evolution of this concept. 'On Narcissism: an Introduction' (1914) widens the scope of the concept by positing an ego libido, or narcissistic libido, besides an object libido.

This is the point at which Freud's work confronts the problem of libidinal economy, a sexual energy which cathects or counter-cathects the ego or object. A summary of the theory of the libido is given in Lecture 26 of the *Introductory Lectures on Psychoanalysis* (1916–17), and in the paper 'The Libido Theory' (1922, *S.E.*, *18*, 255). The economic standpoint, which is concerned with the quantitative aspect of things, is clearly inseparable from the concept of libido. Although the economic standpoint is ever-present in Freudian theory, it cannot be entirely separated from the topographical and dynamic standpoints.

The topographical standpoint implies a systematic description of the different systems or agencies of the psychic apparatus which can, metaphorically, be thought of in *spatial* terms. The two major Freudian topographies are, firstly, the conscious, preconscious and unconscious systems; and secondly, the agencies of id, ego and super-ego. The dynamic standpoint relates to the conflict between the agencies. These three standpoints (economic, topographical and dynamic) make up the Freudian metapsychology.

From the outset, Reich accorded a privileged place to the economic standpoint. Well before his introduction to psychoanalysis he was an 'angry Bergsonian', full of 'life force' (*The Function of the Orgasm*, 1927). In 1919 he wrote a sexological paper, 'The Concept of the Libido from Forel to Jung', published in 1921, in which he compares the libido to an electric current, prefiguring his later research (in Oslo, 1935) into sexual energy as bioelectricity. It is worth recalling that his first presentation to the Vienna Psychoanalytic Society was on 'Libidinal Conflict and the Formation of Delusion in *Peer Gynt*', and that he then drafted a study entitled 'On the Energy of the Drives', then one 'On Genitality', complemented by 'Further Remarks on the Genital Libido'. All this resulted in the first draft of *The Function of the Orgasm*, which contains, as de Marchi rightly claims:

> Not only the reasons for the conflict which placed Reich in opposition to the clinical and pathological theories of orthodox psychoanalysis, but also the later developments of Reichian thought on all three of the sociopolitical, biological and physical levels (de Marchi, 1973, 22). [de Marchi agrees with Reich on this.]

127

The last of these works, *The Function of the Orgasm*, dedicated to Freud, shows very clearly the extent to which his theory differs radically from Freud's. In fact, it is based entirely on the concept of 'actual neurosis' which Freud had introduced in 1898 when differentiating between 'neurasthenia', 'anxiety neurosis' and the psychoneuroses. Neurasthenia was seen as being caused by an actual difficulty in the discharge of sexuality, due, for example, to *coitus interruptus*, and manifested in vague somatic symptoms: generalized pain, headaches, fatigue. The psychoneuroses (hysteria, phobias, obsessional neurosis) are bound to 'significant events in the past' and the symptoms are psychic elaborations, characterized by displacement, symbolization, condensation, etc. They constitute a language which shows us their meaning, when interpreted, as opposed to the somatic symptoms of neurasthenia which are only translations, on the level of the body, of disturbances in the sexual economy. The concept of actual neurosis is only used by Freud to designate a specific syndrome in which a sexual disturbance is purely circumstantial and independent of internal conflict. In the psychoneuroses there are, alongside the symptoms produced by psychic elaboration, disturbances which are similar to those found in actual neurosis. These disturbances, however, are connected to the internal conflict, produced from 'significant events in the past', which impede unconscious wishes from finding expression, and causing libidinal congestion.

128

However, in *The Function of the Orgasm* (1927), Reich extends the concept of actual neurosis to include all psychic disturbances. Disturbances are no longer linked to internal conflicts with roots in childhood, but to simple unsatisfied desire in adult sexuality resulting from purely exogenous factors. The individual, constrained by social prohibitions, is unable to abandon himself to orgasm, to discharge sexual energy. This energy then accumulates, producing a stasis, which has a detrimental effect on the individual's health.

Referring to Freud's *Three Essays*, Reich bemoans the fact that:

Following the rapid progress made by psychoanalysis in its search for the mental causes to the neuroses there has been a loss of interest in 'libidinal stasis', the concept of the somatic origin of neurosis. In Freud's definition it signified an accumulation of the material of sexual chemistry, which produced physical tensions

which were expressed as a drive towards sexual satisfaction . . . Numerous years of the study of the cause,
manifestations and effects of somatic libidinal stasis
lead me to the conviction that the Freudian theory of
actual neurosis . . . is . . . an indispensable part of the
psychopathology and the therapeutic theory of
psychoanalysis.

For Freud, as we saw above, the disturbances which
accompany psychoneurotic symptoms may be related to
undischarged sexual energy, resulting from the repression
of infantile sexual wishes, and when these disturbances
precede the appearance of the psychoneuroses (mainly in
hysteria), they then 'play the part of the grain of sand
which a mollusc coats with layers of mother-of-pearl'
(Freud, 1916, *S.E.*, *16*, 391). According to Reich, it is
simply libidinal stasis which transforms the Oedipus
complex from 'an historical fact to an actual fact'. Freud's
idea of the 'grain of sand' of the actual neuroses forming
the 'core' of certain psychoneuroses should not be confused with Reich's extension of the concept of actual
neurosis to encompass all forms of neurosis. For example,
for Freud, lumbar pain, produced by undischarged sexual
excitation, a sympton of actual neurosis, may appear
before a hysterical conversion. 'The hysteric prefers to use
all the normal or pathological influences which libidinal
excitation exerts on the body to produce his symptoms',
and, similarly, organic illnesses may be used by the condensation and displacements that are characteristic of the
psychoneuroses (the very term emphasizes the mental
activities specific to the neuroses proper, as opposed to the
non-mental or 'actual' neuroses). Figuratively speaking,

129

the hysteric uses these stimuli for the production of symptoms in the same way as the unconscious uses the day's residues for the production of dreams.

According to Reich, anxiety is merely the effect of libidinal stasis, 'and the fear of castration is only given its affective tone of anxiety through somatic libidinal stasis'. Furthermore, unconscious fantasy should be absent during a successful orgasm: 'unconscious imaginary activity becomes useless. Fantasy, by its very nature, is the opposite of lived actuality, as we only imagine that which cannot be obtained in reality'. This idea is radically different from Freud's contention: 'It is my belief that, however strange it may sound, we must reckon with the possibility that something in the nature of the sexual instinct itself is unfavourable to the realization of complete satisfaction' (1912, *S.E.*, *11*, 188).

130

For Freud it is the Oedipus complex which creates the unbridgeable gap between desire and satisfaction, as the original object can never be exactly reproduced in a substitute. Reich, however, believes that objects can be equivalent, which means, according to him, that the subject can avoid idealizing his or her partner. Again we can see a great difference from Freud, who contends that the state of love, and not just coitus, is characterized by idealization. Idealization (overvaluation, overestimation) is, according to Freud, the projection of the ego ideal on to the object, a process which is characteristic of being in love.

The ego ideal is a concept that Freud introduced into psychoanalytic theory at the same time as the concept of narcissism, in 1914. As we noted above, 'man has . . . shown himself incapable of giving up a satisfaction he had once enjoyed' (*S.E.*, *14*, 94); in this case the satisfaction being the feeling of narcissistic perfection experienced by the small child. 'He seeks to recover it in the new form of an ego ideal. What he projects before him as his ideal is the substitute for the lost narcissism of his childhood in which he was his own ideal' (*S.E.*, *14*, 94).

The separation of the subject from the object, the differentiation between ego and non-ego, signal the disintegration of this state of absolute narcissism and its primary feelings of perfection. This disintegration of the egocosmic state is related to the *Hilflosigkeit* mentioned above. Trying to account for the yearning we have for primary narcissism and the consequent idealization of love objects, Freud said, 'Indeed, the primal narcissistic state would not be able to follow the development if it were not for the fact that every individual passes through a period during which he is helpless and has to be looked after, and during which his pressing needs are satisfied by an external agency' (1915, *S.E.*, *14*, 135). It is at this point that the first ego ideal is formed, consisting of a projection (on to the object which is necessary for the powerless ego to survive) of the lost perfection, the (egocosmic) omnipotence that has been undermined.

The helplessness that results from this 'biological factor' of prematurity 'creates the need for love, from which man will never be free'. It also seems to be at the root of our need to love, in order to find one's own lost perfection in the love object. Being close to the idealized object means enacting the fantasy of being reintegrated into a narcissistic whole, as before the time when objects existed as separate and different from the self. The state of being in love is based on the hope of returning to the state when

131

the ego 'was his own ideal'; in love, the ego and the object are fused into a single entity.

According to Freud, the state of being in love is inevitably tied to the idealization of the love object. As well as being related to the earliest stages of life it is also determined by the Oedipus complex: 'The trait of overvaluing the loved one, and regarding her as unique and irreplaceable, can be seen to fall just as naturally into the context of the child's experience, for no one possesses more than one mother, and the relation to her is based on an event that is not open to any doubt and cannot be repeated' ('Contributions to the Psychology of Love'; 1910, *S.E.*, *11*, 169). So, for Freud, the love life of man will be forever coloured by his infancy, in so far as it differs from that of other animals by virtue of prematurity and the incest taboo. Because of this fact it is doomed to a certain measure of dissatisfaction, quite apart from the specific conflicts that beset it. Such a view of the human condition might be considered rather pessimistic were it not for the fact that, elsewhere in Freud's work, this insatiability which characterizes human beings is seen as the motivation for, and even the condition of, our progress. 'It is the difference in amount between the pleasure of the satisfaction which is demanded and that which is actually achieved that provides the driving factor which will permit of no halting at any position attained, but, in the poet's words, "Presses ever forward unsubdued"' (*Beyond the Pleasure Principle*; 1920, *S.E.*, *18*, 42).

From the outset it is clear that Reich's 'optimistism' results from the emphasis he gives to 'actual neurosis' and libidinal stasis. If orgasmic discharge can be adequately achieved, if genitality is unhampered by external con-

132

straints, infantile conflicts need play no part, they are overcome by the realization of genital primacy. De Marchi comments on this point:

> Already, by this time, Reich insisted on an 'energetic' conception of neurosis; which was thought to be the result of determined charges of a physical nature. In this we can see his future orgonomic theory prefigured. He openly admitted that this conception came much closer to the Freudian theory of the actual neuroses (attributed to an 'accumulation' or, as Reich called it, a 'stasis' of sexual energy which was congested because of difficulties in the adult's sexual activity) than to the orthodox doctrine which sees the fundamental cause of neurotic disturbance in such and such an infantile 'fixation' or even in a conflict inherent in the human instinctual dynamic.

133

De Marchi seems to have grasped the essence of Freud's theory, even if he has not understood the full significance of that. In this respect he resembles the rest of the Reichian authors we have come across.

The idea that prohibition comes from outside is found as early as in *The Function of The Orgasm*, which was subtitled 'A Contribution to Psychopathology and the Sociology of Sexual Life'. Aggression and sadism are not considered to be instinctual, nor related to infantile conflicts:

> If the sexual instinct is not satisfied the destructive drive is augmented . . . So if the repression of genitality, and especially the lack of genital satisfaction, increases sadistic drives we must conclude that the general nega-

tion of sexuality *by society* and the dominant tendency to suppress and split it play an important part in the manifestation of sadism in man. [Our italics.]

According to Reich, 'It is the repression of genital tendencies that provokes the irruption of brutality in history', and he classifies the medieval masochistic orgies, the Inquisition, the meetings of German students' associations, and wars, amongst the manifestations of this process. In this book Reich claims that the proletariat is less influenced, in their genitality, than the bourgeoisie: 'The genitality of the proletariat is not hampered by the restrictions issuing from economic interests and those of property relations. And this genitality is all the less inhibited by the worst economic conditions; neuroses are relatively rare among the proletariat.' This conclusion was totally reversed when Reich later claimed that the masses were subject to severe 'sexual misery'.

134

On the other hand, what we find running through all the stages of Reich's work is the disappearance of the concept of internal conflict, and its replacement with the concept of purely external constraints. As we have seen, from the very start Reich's conception is purely economic; the other two standpoints of Freudian metapsychology, described above, being either absent or profoundly altered. This is certainly true of the topographical standpoint, the different agencies of the psychical apparatus, because even if Reich formally employs the terms id, ego and superego, the meaning of these agencies is greatly changed in a system which only acknowledges external prohibitions. The superego, heir to the Oedipus complex, is related to castration anxiety, whereas Reich considers even castration anxiety to be of external origin since the libidinal stasis which causes it comes from the social constraints opposing the genital and orgasmic functions. As for the dynamic standpoint, it has been completely erased because all internal conflict has been made to disappear. Thus, sexual disturbances are severed from their infantile roots, or are seen to have only actual causes. In his first book Reich sowed the seeds of concepts which came to fruition in his later works, and which he summed up in *Reich Speaks of Freud* in the following words: '*You see that it is not possible to broach the problems of mental illness with ideas like the Oedipus complex . . . the main thing is frustration, the genital frustration of the population*' [Reich's italics.] Such a statement cannot be seen as simply polemical, it is an utter rejection of the 'nucleus of the neuroses' as Freud called the Oedipus complex. The absence of the dynamic and topographical standpoints, the disavowal of infantile sexuality, the emphasis placed on quantity at the expense of meaning, all these things add up to an annihilation of the Freudian concept of the unconscious and the significance of Freud's discoveries.

135

Freud was well aware of this. Not only was the gift of Reich's book, which is dedicated to him, coldly received, *The Function of the Orgasm* being one of a series of works which presaged certain later views; but also, two months later, he wrote Reich the following brief note. The note implies a negative criticism of the book's basic thesis – that the treatment of disturbances of the genital orgasmic function (as an aetiological factor) cannot be applied to the psychoneuroses more widely:

Dear Dr Reich,

I have taken considerable time, but have finally read
the manuscript which you dedicated to me in commem-
oration of my birthday. I find the work valuable, rich in
clinical material as well as in ideas. You know that I am
definitely not opposed to your attempt at a solution
which traces neurasthenia back to an absence of genital
primacy . . .

Some authors, examining Reich's works, credit him with
having invented a 'theory of the sexual origin of the neuroses'. Clearly there is some confusion over the use of the
term 'sexual'. The theory in question is undoubtedly
Freud's. Freudian concepts can only be understood, as we
have demonstrated, in the context of his extended concept
of sexuality. The sexual, for Freud, cannot be reduced to
the genital, precisely because of the importance he
accords to infantile sexuality and the partial drives:

136

> In psychoanalytic practice and theory, sexuality does
> not mean only the activities and pleasure which depend
> on the functioning of the genital apparatus: it also
> embraces a whole range of excitations and activities
> which may be observed from infancy onwards and
> which produce a pleasure which cannot be adequately
> explained in terms of the satisfaction of a basic physio-
> logical need (respiration, hunger, excretory function,
> etc.); these re-emerge as component factors in the
> so-called normal form of sexual love (Laplanche &
> Pontalis, 418).

What Reich calls the sexual aetiology of the neuroses is, in
fact, a genital aetiology. It is actually a regression from the
Freudian extension of the concept of sexuality.

Once again, let us note that, well before his exclusion

from the International Psychoanalytic Association in 1934, the 'deviationism' was evident in Reich's theories. And this deviation was quite independent of his political ideas, towards which it led.

These views are taken up again in the second chapter of *Character Analysis*, a chapter which is undated, although the preface indicates that the first parts of the book date from 1928:

> The cardinal importance of genitality, or orgastic impotence, for the aetiology of the neuroses was presented in my book *The Function of the Orgasm*. It attained theoretical importance, for characterological investigations also, through its connection with the theory of the 'actual neuroses'. Thus it became suddenly clear where the problem of quantity lay: it could be nothing other than the somatic basis, the 'somatic core of the neuroses', the actual neurosis (stasis neurosis) which develops from the dammed-up libido. That is, the economic problem of the neurosis as well as the therapy of the neurosis was largely in the somatic realm and not accessible except over the somatic contents of the libido concept.
>
> Now one was better prepared to tackle the question as to what has to be added to the making conscious of the unconscious in order to eliminate the symptom. What becomes conscious is only the *meaning*, the ideational content of the symptom . . . Only the establishment of orgastic potency will result in a decisive change, economically speaking . . . That is, in the final analysis the therapeutic agent is an organic process in the sexual metabolism. This process is based on sexual gratification in the genital orgasm. By eliminating the

137

actual neurosis (stasis neurosis), the somatic core of the neurosis, it also eliminates the psychoneurotic superstructure.

We trust that the reader will have no difficulty in recognizing this as a total inversion of Freudian theory. Reich continues:

It goes without saying that shifting the emphasis from sublimation to direct sexual gratification as a therapeutic goal vastly increases the field of our therapeutic possibilities. On the other hand, this shift also brings us face to face with social difficulties which should not be underestimated (13–15).

138

It is unlikely that Reich was aware of the fact that his theory implies a denial of infantile sexuality. There was a period of time during which he was careful about Freudian doctrine, to which he claimed allegiance, and sometimes made perfectly 'Freudian' statements; for instance: 'Given that the systematic interpretation of behaviour opens up access to the infantile origins of the neuroses another question arises: are there criteria for the choice of the right moment to link actual material to its infantile prototypes? It is understood that this connection is one of the fundamental goals of analysis' (Ch. IV). And: 'Infantile fixation hinders the orgasmic function, which in turn provokes libidinal stasis; the libido thus accumulated intensifies the pregenital fixations, and so on' (Ch. VIII). But then, in the same chapter, Reich explains infantile fixations themselves as being purely and simply the result of the conflict between the drives of the organism and 'the frustrations deriving from the environment'. Even more

unequivocally than in *The Function of the Orgasm* he posits
the superego as being a result of purely external constraints and does not even mention its oedipal origins:
'The ego . . . introjects the frustrating objects of the outer
world which then form the superego. The morals of the
ego, then, do not derive from the id, from the narcissistic
libidinal organism; rather they are a foreign body taken
from the threatening and prohibiting outer world' (159).

Freud's concept is very different: 'Whereas the ego is
essentially the representative of the external world, of
reality, the superego stands in contrast to it as the representative of the internal world of the id . . . The way in
which the superego came into being explains how it is that   *139*
the early conflicts of the ego with the object-cathexes of
the id can be continued in conflicts with their heir, the
superego' (Freud, 1923, *S.E.*, *19*, 36–8).

Reich's purely exogenous concept of the superego leads
him to envisage a society in which morality could be, quite
simply, non-existent:

> It is easy to see that the finding of these mechanisms
> provides the basis for a fundamental criticism of all
> theories of morals. We are dealing here with a decisive
> question of social culture formation. To the extent to
> which the gratification of needs becomes underwritten
> by society, and human structure changes accordingly,
> *moral* regulation of social life will become unnecessary.
> The final decision does not lie in the psychological, but
> in the social realm (172).

Furthermore, the genital character 'is without guilt'. Here
we can see the full extent to which the themes so central to

Freudianism are completely absent from this conception of morality. It is thus completely severed from its infantile and biological bases:

> If we consider once more the origin of the superego as we have described it, we shall recognize that it is the outcome of two highly important biological factors: namely, the lengthy duration in man of his childhood helplessness and dependence, and the fact of his Oedipus complex (Freud, 1923, *S.E.*, *19*, 35).

To imagine that society can satisfy all our needs is to deny the extent of the infantile within us, of our early helplessness, and of our unassuageable incestuous desires. It is interesting that Reich even manages to find an external reason for early helplessness: 'The child is crushed by parental authority because he is physically small' (*The Sexual Revolution*, 79).

Before long, however, the repudiation of the role of infantile sexuality in mental processes becomes completely conscious and confirmed. Although it is difficult to date, with precision, the various chapters of *The Sexual Revolution*, which were written between 1930 and 1936, we will use a few quotations from this work. In a section called 'The Triangular Structure' Reich claims that: 'There would be no repression if the boy had to give up his mother but would be allowed to masturbate and play genital games with children of his age' (78). We will return to the long-term consequences of this 'permissive' style of upbringing. What interests us here is the way in which psychic economy is being made to supplant, in a definite and unequivocal way, the entire space of the metapsychology. Sexuality is seen as an energy, and nothing but. It needs only to be allowed to flow naturally and the Oedipus complex will vanish.

In this same book this concept is further refined:

> Briefly summarized, psychoanalytic investigation of the unconscious motives of the conflict at puberty has shown a reactivation of early infantile incestuous desires and sexual guilt feelings which in reality correspond to unconscious fantasies and not to the act of masturbation.
>
> Orgasm research, however, has found that masturbation is caused not by incestuous desires but by sexual excitation which corresponds to the heightened activity of the sexual apparatus. It is only sexual stasis that revives the old incest fantasy . . . Unless regression has been conditioned earlier by a pathological fixation in childhood, it is exclusively a consequence of the social denial of genital gratification at the time of maturity (85–6).

141

The small concession to Freudian concepts ('unless this regression has been conditioned earlier by a pathological fixation in childhood') does not stop us recognizing Reich's theory, as it will be expressed later, in its essence here: 'If you can imagine a current, a natural current, you have to let it flow. If you obstruct it with a dam, it overflows, that's all' (Reich, 1952, 85).

It is, in fact, all; this hydraulic metaphor indicates that if the downstream flow is blocked it will start to flow back upstream, with a recathexis of the sequence of 'the forms and objects of early and infantile sexuality', which would have played no part in it otherwise. Regression, perversion, delinquency are all the effects of this damming up of energy which resexualizes the infantile positions. Later Reich was to add all sorts of organic illnesses to the list of the effects of the damming up of the libido, most importantly, cancer.

Meanwhile, in a chapter called 'A Note on the Basic Conflict between Need and the Outer World', which concludes the first edition of *Character Analysis* (Ch. XIII, third edition), Reich puts forward the hypothesis that:

> Psychic energy derives from simple physiological and mechanical surface tensions which are formed in the various tissues, particularly the vegetative system and the blood and lymph system. The disturbance of the physico-chemical equilibrium produced by these tensions, then, would be the motor power behind actions and, in the last analysis, also, behind thinking (282).

142

This theory, which is a mere fantasy on the organic level, dispenses with the instincts, the drives, their sources (the erogenous zones), the stages (oral, anal, etc.) and, definitively, with any Freudian theory of the psyche.

Despite Reich's claim, in the preface to the second edition of this book, that 'character analysis is as fully valid in the framework of depth-psychological thinking as of the *psycho*therapeutics which correspond to it' (18), we can see the gulf that actually separates the Reichian from the Freudian theories.

In the first chapter of the second edition (Chapter XIV), Reich notifies the reader that 'this monograph is an expansion of a paper read at the 13th International Psychoanalytic Congress in Lucerne, August 1934'. (Remember that it was this Congress that marked Reich's expulsion from the International Psychoanalytic Associa-

tion.) Although it is difficult to tell what may be a 1935
addition to the 1934 text, the monograph contains such
statements as:

> Previously, the fact that modern man has an Oedipus
> complex was considered an explanation of his neurotic
> illness. Today, this thesis, while not given up, is of
> relative importance: The child–parent conflict becomes
> pathogenic only as a result of disturbed sexual economy
> on the part of the child . . . It became less important
> whether, early in the analysis, one obtained much or
> little material, whether one learned much or little about
> the patient's past. The decisive question came to be
> whether one obtained, in a correct fashion, those
> experiences which represented concentrations of vege-
> tative energy (301).

143

In *Dialectical Materialism and Psychoanalysis*, written in
1929, Reich tries to make the Oedipus complex compatible with Marxism. This results, among other things, in
turning the complex into a purely contingent and historical factor:

> Translated into the language of sociology, Freud's cen-
> tral thesis concerning the importance of the Oedipus
> complex in the development of the individual means
> precisely that social being determines that develop-
> ment. The child's instincts and disposition – empty
> moulds ready to receive their social contents – go
> through the (social) processes of relationships with
> father, mother and teacher, and only then acquire their
> final form and content (40).

Furthermore:

The Oedipus complex must disappear in a socialist society because its social basis – the patriarchal family – will itself disappear, having lost its *raison d'être*. Communal upbringing, which forms part of the socialist program, will be so unfavourable to the forming of psychological attitudes as they exist within the family today – the relationship of children to one another and to the persons who bring them up will be so much more many sided, complex and dynamic – that the Oedipus complex . . . will lose its meaning . . . It also means that the Oedipus complex is regarded as a fact which in the last analysis is economically determined and, at least in the form which it assumes, socially determined (46).

144

But, in fact, it is in *The Invasion of Compulsory Sex Morality* (1931) that Reich, using Malinowski's study of the Trobriand Islanders, *The Sexual Life of Savages* (1929), sounds the death-knell of what Freud called the nucleus of the neuroses:

Now it has been shown that among Trobrianders the parents' attitude not only is not disturbing but is rather friendly and benevolent. We can say, therefore, that, with the exception of the incest taboo, there is no sex-negating morality . . . As sexuality is free, the incest taboo cannot be considered a sexual restriction since abundant possibilities for gratification of a sex-economic nature remain. One cannot speak of a restriction of *the gratification of the food instinct if the eating of mutton and green peas is banned but the person can eat as much of any other vegetable or meat as he pleases* . . .

We italicize these lines because this attempt to reduce incest wishes, which are at the foundation of the psyche according to Freud, to a question of eating mutton or peas has a distinct flavour . . . dare we say that it smacks of a regression from the Oedipal to oral stages? Anyway, Reich continues:

> An economically and dynamically excessive incest wish is found where there is too great an interest in the incestuous object because of a general restriction of instinctual life. This is true of all other excessive instinctual impulses and explains the fact that the primitive is quite conscious of the incest *prohibition* but it need not be repressed because the incest *wish* does not particularly stand out from other desires as long as the other desires are satisfied (7–9).

145

Once again, rather simplistically, Reich ignores meaning in favour of the economic standpoint, and denies infantile sexuality in favour of genitality. We might also wonder how it is that a psychoanalyst, or even an anthropologist, could fail to question this apparent tolerance for every form of sexuality save incest. Is it not absolutely obvious that incest wishes play a slightly different part from the desire to have mutton and peas for dinner? When Reich claims that incest wishes are conscious in primitive societies (and here he is extending Malinowski's observations on the Trobriand Islanders to include all primitive societies 'in general'), this only applies to sibling incest, but not to the mother–son relation. Moreover, the extent of consciousness of incest wishes is very difficult to ascertain. In many Eastern European countries, especially Russia, the supreme insult is to tell someone to go fuck their mother. Is this to say that the incest wishes are conscious? The idea has crossed the barrier of censorship only because it has been considerably deformed, especially in favour of an anal-sadistic regression. Reich writes on: 'If the greater part of society lives sex-economically, there can be no neuroses, simply because these disorders arise from an inhibited genital life. That is the conclusion we must reach if we follow consistently the libido theory and the theory of the neuroses' (28). As is often the case, Reich tends to attribute to 'psychoanalysis' theories which are of his own making. Psychoanalysis says the exact opposite: it is the neurotic conflict which dis-

146 turbs genitality. In a footnote Reich recognizes, for once, that his conception of the neuroses is 'rejected by Freud and his school'. According to Reich, who fully endorses Malinowski's observations, perversions do not exist among the Trobriand Islanders; thanks once again to the free flow of sexuality through its outlet of genitality, unconstrained by family and society. Oddly enough, he takes up his alimentary metaphor again, when discussing the perversions: 'He despises perversions as he despises one who eats inferior or impure things instead of good clean food' (29).

We will return to Reich's attack on the family, marriage and patriarchal society, which is seen to lie at the heart of 'the invasion of compulsory sex morality'. But it must be pointed out that he can find no psychological explanation for the 'conjugal morality' and constraints imposed on young newlyweds in Trobriand society. We know that Malinowski was trying to disprove the universality of the Oedipus complex in his book. Trobriand society was depicted as matriarchal (when it is, in fact, merely matrilineal). Their marriage is patrilocal. Ultimately, the power returns to the men. The tribal chief is always a man, and inside the family it is the mother's brother who represents him.[9] The family structure would lead to the exclusion of the Oedipus complex. The part played by the father in procreation is 'unknown' and the mother's brother takes on those functions that our society considers paternal. Malinowski takes this apparent ignorance of paternity as real, and the Oedipus complex as a phenomenon resulting from the Western model of the family, without viewing it as a structure which may assume different forms. Reich imagines that the institution of bridewealth (which usually comprises yams grown by the bride's brothers) heralds the demise of matriarchal society and introduces sexual prohibitions. Young newlyweds are very constrained in comparison to their premarital sex life and must avoid any public expressions of tenderness. 'The grossest and most unpardonable form of swearing or insult are the words: *Kwoy um kwava* (Go copulate with your wife), which lead to murder, suicide or sorcery.' The marriage demands absolute fidelity. According to Reich, this 'irruption of morality' is the result of economics (the bridewealth) which, being given to the husband, signifies the transition to patriarchy.

Indeed we do not want to trivialize the role of yams in all this business and, for sure, marriage makes things comfortable for men, but it seems unlikely that this economic factor could have been at the root of prohibitions that are applied to both man and wife. Why should 'Go copulate with your wife' be the supreme insult? Is it perhaps a substitute for the other insult, mentioned earlier, 'go fuck your mother'? In other words, it may be that

147

marriage takes on an oedipal significance with incestuous meaning, which is increased since the role of the father is considered to be unknown. What has to be suppressed in order for there to be 'ignorance' of paternity is the fact that a sexual relation exists between mother and father. So, in turn, they try to behave as if sex between husband and wife did not exist. The type of defence employed by this tribe against the Oedipus complex includes a specific set of prohibitions directed against anything which endangers that defence, which nevertheless remains extremely fragile since, according to both Reich and Malinowski, the Trobrianders try to calculate their inheritance laws through a paternal lineage. Yet, if a man is thought to be 'ignorant' of the fact that his wife's child is his own, how can paternal inheritance and bridewealth be the basis of all social institutions, especially this type of marriage? The more fragile the defence the more rituals and taboos are necessary to shore it up. So, can we really imagine that all these complicated psychosexual prohibitions, the murders, suicides and sorcery all exist because of some yams . . . ?

148

In fact, marriage always carries deeply oedipal meanings, even if it was, perhaps, originally based on economic factors. We have only one father and one mother, and marriage contains the symbolic representation of a union with one of the parents. Polygamy is a regression from the Oedipus complex, a form of revenge on mother; for if she was unique for the child, she nevertheless had a husband to herself and often had other children too.[10]

Our interpretation of the prohibitions and constraints on married couples may be wrong. After all we have never met the Trobriand Islanders – neither had Reich for that matter. But what we have suggested is a hypothesis which takes account of Freudian discoveries: of infantile sexuality, of the Oedipus complex, and of the primacy of internal factors (conflict). We have assumed that behaviour is the result of conflict between the drives and the defences against those drives; in short, we think that psychic phenomena and their effects have a significance that cannot be reduced to a particular energy. If we try to take account of meaning without energy we have only a partial explanation of the question in hand. To do this provides an inadequate means of clinical evaluation, renders therapeutic practice ineffectual, and ultimately risks turning psychoanalysis into an intellectual game. But to account for energy without considering meaning irretrievably undermines the scope of the Freudian discovery, and actually constitutes a regression to pre-Freudianism.

149

Of whom might the following remark be expected, a psychoanalyst or a nineteenth-century neurologist? 'Ejaculation is totally explicable as a reflex action of the spinal centre which is set off by friction as sensory excitation. And the friction itself can be no more explained than can the scratching of a cutaneous itch, unless we should give a psychological explanation of physiology.' This is Reich's reply, in *The Function of the Orgasm*, to Ferenczi's brilliant theory of amphimixis. In his book *Thalassa: A Theory of Genitality* (1924), Ferenczi describes the way that genital coitus, in man, results from a successful synthesis of several pregenital components. In cases where this fails, or where one of the partial drives dominates the others, the result is that the sexual function is disturbed (such as in impotence, premature ejaculation, etc.).

Ferenczi gives a clinical description of each of these disturbances and of the mechanisms corresponding to the level of the various partial drives.

Reich's rejection of meaning can be compared to a phenomenon described, by our colleagues at the French school of psychosomatic medicine, as 'operational thought'. According to them, this process is characteristic of some psychosomatic patients who seem to show a lack of fantasizing. Clinical observation has shown a similar kind of thinking in certain pre-psychotic patients. It seems, at first sight, as if there are such strong defences that the conscious mind is completely severed from the unconscious. It is as if the products of the unconscious are not reaching the surface, as if the primary processes are totally cut off from the secondary processes, and the pleasure principle is completely divorced from the reality principle. These patients give the impression of perfectly rational and completely coherent thinking; one feels that it is too perfect a rationality and too total a coherence. The subjects who manifest this kind of thinking often go on to produce the systematic delusions of paranoia, or to develop increasingly rigid character traits. A deeper examination shows that what seemed to be 'operational thought' was actually a vast secondary revision, a great rationalization of drives and their defences. The pressure that the unconscious exerts on consciousness, and its irruption into consciousness, is veiled by a fabric woven of the very material it is supposed to hide. The screen is made up of the very stuff it is supposed to conceal.

Similarly, in Reich's work the meaning which would seem to have been banished ends up by returning in the guise of the pursuer himself. Eventually, it is the concept of energy (the libido, sexual energy) which comes to be seen as completely charged with meaning. This is really an economic validation of a psychoanalytic adage which, although it has never been formalized, is nevertheless implicit in Freudian theory: 'Banish meaning, it comes flooding back'. As regards the possible correlation between some paranoid mechanisms and the 'operational thought' of psychosomatic patients, this is not the place for such an investigation. It is simply worth noting, without drawing any conclusions from it, that Reich manifested a range of problems alongside his psychosis: eczema, tuberculosis and a propensity for alcoholism. So when in 1942, in the second edition of *The Function of the Orgasm*, Reich stated that, 'whilst most analysts attributed everything to the psychic contents of neurotic symptoms, eminent psychopathologists such as Jaspers claimed that psychological analyses of meaning, and consequently psychoanalysis, had strayed right out of the sphere of natural science', and when he claimed that, with his conception of energy, 'for the first time in the history of psychology' he had placed the latter within the sphere of the natural sciences, it was already too late to believe him, for he had discovered orgone.

We feel that the authors of *Anti-Oedipus*, although they often quote him, do not do Reich justice. There is, in fact, a direct affiliation between his ideas and their own.[11] Without making any claims for being able to make a complete parallel between 'anti-oedipal' theses and Reichian theses, the following similarities are not hard to spot.

One of the fundamental criticisms that Deleuze & Guattari make of psychoanalysis is that it sees the uncon-

scious as being a theatre, when it is really a factory: 'a
classical theatre was substituted for the unconscious as a
factory; representation was substituted for the units of
production of the unconscious; and an unconscious that
was capable of nothing but expressing itself – in myth,
tragedy, dreams – was substituted for the productive
unconscious' (24). Throughout the entire book the
authors assert that the unconscious doesn't mean anything [ne veut rien dire], that it only produces. Such a view is
a repetition of Reich's attempt to banish meaning in order
to have a purely economic metapsychology. Isn't it
another way of saying that 'life simply functions, that it
has no meaning?' (Reich, 1942, 210).

152

One of the main themes of Anti-Oedipus is 'familialism',
which is a creation of psychoanalysis in alliance with
capitalism, intended to deprive man, or at least European
man, of his revolutionary powers of desire: 'psychoanalysis is taking part in the work of bourgeois repression
at its most far-reaching level, that is to say, keeping European humanity harnessed to the yoke of daddy-mommy
and making no effort to do away with this problem once
and for all' (50). The book is an attempt at formulating a
final solution to the daddy-mommy problem, and in it we
find that to do away with the problem and 'to do away
with Freud' amount to pretty much the same thing. We
have not yet described Reichian attacks on the family, but
his are not a patch on Deleuze & Guattari's. But of
significance here is that one of the versions of what Reich
called the 'emotional plague' was 'familitis', or the
malady of the family.

According to the authors of Anti-Oedipus, Freud recoiled
when he came face to face with 'explosive desire and the

savage world of production', and tried to lock away 'the unconscious into the family triangle'.

> It is as though Freud were asking to be forgiven his profound discovery of sexuality by saying to us: at least it won't go any further than the family! The dirty little secret, in place of the wide open spaces glimpsed for a moment. The familialist reduction, in place of the drift of desire. In place of the great decoded flows, little streams recoded in mommy's bed (270).

In the end there is not much difference between this version and Reich's concept of energy in terms of the 'actual neurosis'. We have seen that, for Reich, it is society (capitalist-bourgeois) that prevents sexual energy from being freely discharged through the genital orgasmic outlet (and we will explore these Reichian theses in greater detail). When the flow is blocked in its downstream direction (even the hydraulic metaphor is already there), a flowback will cause the recathexis of past objects, particularly the Oedipus complex. One of Deleuze & Guattari's propositions is an exact repetition of this formula: 'If desire is repressed this is not because it is the desire of the mother and for the death of the father; on the contrary, it only becomes this because it is repressed.' But one difference that exists between these dissidents is that Reich did not immediately dismiss Freud as being in cahoots with bourgeois society, but later came to criticize psychoanalysis for contributing to the suppression of the sexual rights of young people, and to criticize Freud for being the defender of 'civilization' at the expense of the renunciation of instinctual satisfaction.

Also Deleuze & Guattari never tire of proclaiming that

FREUD OR REICH?   [CH.

parents are insignificant objects: 'the parental figures are
in no way organizers but rather inductors or stimuli of
varying, vague import' (91). This idea is not far from
Reich's contention that it is only because of prohibited
genitality that the incest taboo is of any greater significance than a dietary prohibition on mutton stew. By
claiming that the Oedipus complex is a product of the
socio-economic organization of society, by increasingly
curtailing its scope, Reich paved the way for the 'anti-
oedipals'.

As for delusion, it is seen as having a 'world-historical,
political, racial content'. This theme recurs throughout
154   *Anti-Oedipus*:

> All delirium possesses a world-historical, political and
> racial content, mixing and sweeping along races, cul-
> tures, continents, and kingdoms; some wonder whether
> this long drift merely constitutes a derivative of
> Oedipus. The familial order explodes, families are chal-
> lenged, son, father, mother, sister – it is a question of
> knowing if the historico-political, the racial and the
> cultural are merely part of a manifest content and
> formally depend on a work of elaboration, or if, on the
> contrary, this content should be followed as the thread
> of latency that the order of families hides from us
> (88–9).

There is a case study of Reich's, dating from the
orgonomic period (1948), which shows that his interpretation is very similar to Deleuze & Guattari's,
although rather less poetic or romantic. The similarity lies
in the fact that he does not analyse the contents of the
unconscious, the drives that take the parental figures as

their objects, but instead takes the speech of mentally
disturbed subjects as revelatory of social truths. This is an
extract from an interesting case:

> Thursday November 19,1942.
> It is awful and I don't know what to do. The other night
> I found out the why of the world and the war and almost
> everything. They were drinking gallons of blood in
> front of me. The devil is red because of that and he gets
> redder and redder and then the dripping blood on the
> mass by drops and this was being swallowed then he
> was seated by the side of the devil and drinking too – the
> table was round oblong of flowing thick blood (no feet
> on it) Mother Mary was at the corner watching. She
> was as white as a sheet – All her blood had been drained
> off and consumed. She saw her son drinking that and
> suffered. I did not want to see it or hear it or know the
> why of everything – that why but they force me to see
> and hear – Maybe because of Isis – whom they used all
> those thousands of years in between I don't know what
> to do. ('The Schizophrenic Split', Ch. XVI, *Character
> Analysis*, 501).

155

'The other night I found out the why of the world and the
war and almost everything. They were drinking gallons of
blood in front of me.' *This statement was perfectly true, in full
accordance with reality*: Hitler and the other militarists were
shedding millions of gallons of blood (Reich's comment,
502).

> 14 February 1943
> Things are screwy as hell – the world and all the people
> in it stink – Everybody is out to cut everybody else's

throat – with large butcher's knives – they kill eight
million – they were the Jews and they keep us here alive
– it makes no sense – nothing does – I'm not supposed to
be eating and I eat so I'm paid back with intrigue and
pettiness – All around me – Just to trap me in the
middle of it all – I have to be 115 lb. – For a long time
now and I get close to it and then eat tons and gain it all
back – the ten disciples are still waiting to be taken out
of the catacombs and I can't draw them out until I'm
115 lb. – Now they are with the right-hand side – The
Lord and they help me on my promise not to eat but I
do eat and, as I said before, get paid back plenty – so
156   much that I can't always cope with it all. I don't know
anybody today only about generations ago – centuries
ago – eons ago – ancient sage –

Only work today is *right* and *real* – I love it – it never fails
you – never – the work is a straight line.

You told my brother you would write – please, please
do – I don't know anything and I'd like to hear about
the straight corners from you – Thanks a lot – F (503).

Reich comments:

Great insight into the realities of our society and our
ways of life, though expressed in a distorted manner,
was characteristic of this letter too, and is the way in
which many a schizophrenic looks through us (503).

Reich does not mention the overtly cannibalistic elements
of the patient's drives, the object of these drives (the virgin
mother whose son drinks her blood), or the butcher's
knives in relation to the drives, or the guilt about eating,

etc. Finally, no mention is made of the transference (millions of Jews killed). A psychoanalyst takes the events of the real world (war, murder of Jews) into account, when trying to understand the delusion in an illness, to the extent that these represent elements that activate unconscious drives (see Klein, 1961). We suggested earlier, in a different context, that these can be understood as playing a part similar to that of the day's residues in the formation of a dream.

To Reich, as to Deleuze & Guattari, the schizophrenic seems to be a superior kind of creature, whilst '*homo normalis*' (for Reich) and the neurotic (for Deleuze & Guattari, and at least we seem to have some progress over the intervening years) are despised as fearful people who have not dared to let loose and drift out to the open sea:

> I know today that mental patients experience this consonance without differentiating between self and world, and that the average citizen has no inkling of consonance and merely experiences his beloved ego as a sharply delineated centre of the world (*The Function of the Orgasm*, 43).

> Mental patients often conceive of locking up their attendants and physicians as the ones who are really sick. It is they who are in the right not the others. This idea is not as fanciful as one would like to believe (69).

> With respect to their experiencing of life, the neurotic patient and the perverted individual are to the schizophrenic as the petty thief is to the daring safecracker (70).

157

FREUD OR REICH?   [CH.

Later we shall see that this lucidity of intelligence in the schizophrenic is one of the major dangers which threaten his existence in present-day society (*Character Analysis*, 413).

In schizophrenic experiences the world which is called 'The Beyond' in common mysticism and in true religion manifests itself before our eyes. One must learn to read this language. What is never admitted by *homo normalis*, what is lived out only clandestinely or laughed at in a silly manner, are the seriously disturbed forces of nature (461).

158   This schizophrenic, who has managed to cast off his narrow ego, reappears in *Anti-Oedipus*:

The ego, however, is like daddy-mommy: the schizo has long since ceased to believe in it (23).
Schizophrenia teaches us a singular extra-oedipal lesson, and reveals to us an unknown force of the disjunctive synthesis, an imminent use that would no longer be exclusive or restrictive, but fully affirmative, non-restrictive, inclusive. A disjunction that remains disjunctive, and that still affirms the disjoined terms, that affirms them throughout their entire distance, without restricting one by the other or excluding the other from the one, is perhaps the greatest paradox. 'Either . . . or . . . or', instead of 'either/or'. The schizophrenic is not man and woman. He is man or woman, but he belongs precisely to both sides, man on the side of men, woman on the side of women . . . He is child *or* parent, not both, but the one at the end of the other, like the two ends of a stick

in a nondecomposable space . . . He is not simply bisex-
ual, or between the two, or intersexual. He is transsexual.
He is trans-alivedead, trans-parentchild (76–7).

Ego and non-ego, self and not-self, outside and inside,
all these lose their meaning.

Just as the Reichian schizophrenic affords us insight into
the mystic's 'Beyond' and into 'true religion' with his
natural powers, so the Guattaro-Deleuzian schizophrenic
is a 'man-made schizophrenic' whose misunderstood
genius could only have come to fruition in conditions that
have been destroyed by capitalism.

As for the harmony between man and nature, which is   *159*
very important for Deleuze & Guattari, it, too, was sought
by Reich, and not only in the 'consonance' of the schizophrenic, but in all of us. According to him there are some
misguided people who still believe in 'the antithesis
between man and nature', who will never be able to grasp
'the identity of the sexual process to the life process'
(1942). In *Character Analysis* he specifies: 'I am here allud-
ing to those functions which unite man and his cosmic
origin in one whole and unique entity'. And from the
orgonomic period onwards this becomes a central feature
of Reich's work.

Lastly, the 'desiring machines' are also to be found in
Reich's work, not only in the projected forms of orgone
accumulators, but directly in his descriptions of the body:
'All of us are merely a specially organized electric machine
which is correlated with the energy of the cosmos' (1927, 42).

This similarity between Reich's thought and that of

Deleuze & Guattari should not detract from the latter's value and originality. Reich is far from having their imagination, verve and poetic lyricism; and he would be flattered to know that they have attached their plug [*douille voleuse*] to his powerful electrical system.

The author of *The Function of the Orgasm* is also a precursor of the disavowal of infantile sexuality and the substitution of sexuality in the pre-Freudian sense of the word. As in many other things a 'return to Reich' is very much in evidence these days. We have already mentioned one or two of Reich's ideas on education, and these too prefigured a number of pedagogical ideas that have recently been used. We quoted a few paragraphs from *The Sexual Revolution* in which he advocates nudity between parents and children, the freedom of children to play sexual games, and even their being offered the opportunity to be spectators of their parents' sexual antics. In fact, Reich gives two or three clinical examples in which parents are seen as having caused sexual disturbances in their children because of their lack of 'permissiveness'. Also, in his paper on 'The Masochistic Character' (1932, *Character Analysis*, Ch. XI), which was the basis of the conflict we described above, in which he refutes the concept of the death instinct, he describes the case of a patient who is perverse and, it seems, pre-schizophrenic:

> The enormous fear of punishment which prevents the progress to genitality is a result of this contradiction between sexual impulses which are permitted, even encouraged, on the one hand, and impulses which are threatened with severe punishment on the other hand. Our patient was allowed to eat as much as he pleased,

160

in fact he was encouraged to eat much; he was allowed to lie in bed with his mother, to embrace and stroke her; there was much interest in his excretory functions. But when he proceeded to show interest in his mother's genitals and wanted to touch her he met with the full severity of parental authority (228).

It never even occurs to Reich that the patient's problems might have been caused by the 'intimacies' permitted him by the mother rather than by the limits she imposed on them. What crowns it all is that, a few sentences later, Reich blames 'our patriarchal educational system' for 'damage done to the child' when, if anything seems clear about this case, it is the effect of paternal absence; the father seems to have abandoned his function to the son. A few pages later Reich reports:

As late as puberty the patient often slept with his mother in the same bed. At the age of seventeen he developed a phobia about his mother becoming pregnant by him. The closeness to his mother and her body warmth stimulated his masturbation . . . He would follow girls at some distance, having vivid fantasies that they were 'pressing their bellies against each other' and that that would result in pregnancy (239).

Once again, Reich finds it unremarkable that a young man is taking his father's place in his mother's bed. A similar situation was discovered when one of us had to treat a young schizophrenic man. His father had died when he was ten years old and he had shared a bed with his mother until he was sixteen. He had developed a similar fear of making his mother pregnant. He came to

treatment at the age of twenty-four, with many delusional
ideas, including a plan for building a machine to resusci-
tate the dead. He spoke, with enormous anxiety, about his
past fears of making his mother pregnant, and consciously
hated her for having made him take his father's place in
her bed. Resuscitating the dead, of course, meant bringing his father back to life so that he might, amongst other
things, take on his paternal role and separate the son from
his seductive mother. (A question for Deleuze & Guattari,
in passing, was whether this schizophrenic was 'extra-
oedipal' or not?) But, according to Reich, parents and
society should not be merely tolerant but be actively
permissive:

162

> A non-authoritarian society . . . would not content
> itself with not prohibiting an erotic relation between
> two adolescents, for example, but would give it full
> protection. It would not content itself with not prohibit-
> ing masturbation, for example, but would severely
> reprove every adult who prevented a child from
> developing its natural sexuality (7–8).

In *The Invasion of Compulsory Sex Morality* (1931), Reich
demands that parents, educators, psychoanalysts and
society take on their full 'responsibilities'. Having proclaimed the Trobriand Islanders' parental attitude as one
that is not prohibitive of sexual play but full of 'benevolence', he adds in a footnote dated 1934:

> However slight the difference may appear to be
> between mere toleration and the affirmation of infantile
> and pubertal sex-life, it is decisive for the psychic struc-
> ture formation of the child . . . The explicit and

unmistakable affirmation of infantile love-life on the part of educators, however, can become the basis of sex-affirmative elements of ego structure, even when it cannot palliate the social influences. This view is intended as a criticism of the attitude of those psycho-analysts who dare not take the important step from toleration to affirmation. Replying that this has to be left to the children is nothing but a shifting of responsibility.

Well, the damage that is done to children, by attitudes such as those Reich prescribes, makes it impossible for us to agree with him. Firstly, he seems to totally ignore the element of adult *seduction* which is inherent in the policies he advocates; not only in the exhibitionism of nudity and/or sexual relations witnessed by children, but also in adult collusion and complicity. Such activities are a good opportunity for adults to place their perverse desires on the same side as their good conscience. We have come across a 'liberal' father who, when his daughter was pregnant, gave her an abortion. She became severely disturbed. Another 'liberal' father, whose daughter was going on holiday with her boy-friend, gave the young man 'advice' on contraception and bought a douche as a parting gift for the happy holiday-makers. Not only did the young woman become frigid, but her entire psychosexual life was scarred by her 'modern' upbringing, of which this was just the tail-end. A long and difficult treatment has managed to undo some of the effects of such parental 'benevolence'. The 'permissiveness' of parents, and of the psychoanalyst (on another level) for that matter, tends to obstruct the path of desire when such permissiveness is in

163

the form of complicity. Desire requires a lack, or an
obstacle, in order to be created and to develop; we do not
desire that which has already been given to us. A 'permissive' attitude can take on the significance of castration,
depriving the subject of the pleasure in searching for, and
achieving, satisfaction. The child, and the adolescent, is
also afraid of his own drives. The ego feels itself to be
overwhelmed by excitation. Children and adolescents
often need support to help them contain what they experience as feelings which threaten to overwhelm and destroy
the self. Complete permissiveness only exacerbates feelings of insecurity. This may result in an imbalance, or,
164   quite inversely to Reich's claims, in reinforcing the superego, since internal prohibitions will be made all the
stronger in the absence of external ones. Generally speaking, the individual's ability to achieve the genitality which
Reich values so highly will be hampered by too intense a
sexual gratification experienced in childhood.

If we examine some of the pedagogical proposals in the
book *Journal d'un Éducastreur* (1971) by Julien Celma we
can clearly see how they have been influenced by Reichian
ideas, although Reich (consciously) claimed that he was
against the seduction of children by adults.

For those readers who are not avid readers of the tab-
loids and who might be astonished at the quotations we
have taken from the book, or might think them to be
unrepresentative, we would add that *Le Monde* took this
book very seriously, without showing any surprise at the
ideas it contains. Also, these ideas are part of a certain
mentality which you find here and there, and which is
easily unearthed in many other areas of contemporary
life. Let us further add that Celma's book was very suc-

cessful in the shops (our copy is at least a second edition),
a success with the critics who were, doubtless, afraid of
being called reactionary if they failed to praise the scan-
dalous and provocative project. Its success was also due to
the fact that it takes some of the more fashionable ideas on
'sexual liberation' to their logical conclusion, even if it
seems to caricature them by doing so.[12]

Julien Celma was a supply teacher for the academic
year 1968–9. On the book's dustjacket he is quoted as
saying: 'The children and I made some great gestures. At
times we broke completely from the "Old World".' These
great gestures are written up in sixties vocabulary which
borrows from Marx (alienation, dominant ideology),   *165*
from Reich (sexual struggle, sexual misery) and mostly
from Freud (fixation, regression, repression, latency,
transference, Oedipus, etc.). The ideas are themselves
redolent of a particularly sixties ideology (which we, in
turn, feel justified in calling a 'dominant ideology'), with
the usual touch of paranoia, which is, in this case,
especially strong.

For example, you may think that a compulsory and
state funded education is one of the achievements of
democracy and that it represents a victory for social freedom; but if so you are underestimating the insidious
conspiracy of capital:

Let no one be fooled; power is never fooled. Schooling
was made compulsory and free because this solution
corresponded, at one point, to the interest of the bourgeoisie. The economic developments necessitated a better informed worker . . . How could we fail to see the
child's period of schooling as a murder, without count-

ing the family . . . Children are schooled by slaves who
will turn out more slaves, who themselves will turn out
more slaves like electric grinders . . .

If this sounds reminiscent of Strindberg's descriptions of
schooling in *The Servant's Son* (1886), it should be remembered that although he was paranoid he was, nevertheless, a genius. Meanwhile Celma was determined not to
collude in this 'sordid assassination of life', and put into
practice the ideas 'born of the *mai-juinist* movement' of
1968:

> I then had the idea of taking the non-directive tech-
> nique [The class was working, before Celma's arrival,
> under the aegis of the theories of Rogers and C. Freinet]
> a bit further, right up to the complete eradication of all
> directives, all discipline, all moral censorship, every
> part of the teacher's role. I destroyed the last vestiges of
> an already rather battered authority in order to create a
> wider educational experience . . . Then a transforma-
> tion took place in the classroom which showed the
> oppressive nature of even 'non-directive' methods in
> use there . . . Conflicts broke out, battles were fought.
> Chaos. Tension . . . The 'best' pupil of the class became
> 'spiteful', 'lazy' and 'obscene' . . . Schoolwork no
> longer existed, or hardly at all . . . Very soon the rela-
> tions became sexualized. Explicit gestures, allusions.
> All this within a profoundly oedipal emotional climate.
> I was the Grownup, the father with whom incest (and
> murder) could be envisaged.

The author thought that, for the boys, 'the transference
object was not what they wanted no doubt', whereas for

the girls the opposite was true. Thus, Monique, aged nine, 'very pretty, very seductive even', wrote him a letter decorated with hearts which ended 'and I send you a big kiss on the mouth', and which the teacher countersigned: 'before a blushing little face, excited and no doubt happy'. Even if his behaviour was 'perfectly neutral', many desires must have been repressed.

Another experiment involved a class discussion on the merits of coeducation:

> For two hours the three little girls just wouldn't stop; one was stroking my hair, another was buttoning and unbuttoning my cardigan, especially the bottom part, the third was playing with my feet. After two hours I stopped the discussion because I was getting too turned on, and to what end? . . .

167

It was only the morality of dominant ideology that stopped him from taking the desires that had been kindled by this encounter to their conclusion: 'the adult–child relation, seen strictly from the erotic and playful aspect, should be enacted without any kind of inhibition whatsoever (which I did not do) . . .' And also:

> Maintaining non-erotic relations between adults and children, that is between people of different ages, will be considered (in the non-alienated society of tomorrow) as a symptom of a serious illness. The self-censorship of the kids also played a part in this inadequacy. Kids of eight or nine are already to some extent destroyed, and their personalities show a number of neurotic signs (socially adaptive behaviour to a neurotic society). Very strong guilt feelings vied with more authentic

behaviour, with more pleasant implications, non-moralistic behaviour in other words.

These children were so 'alienated' that in one of the classes they wanted, above all else, to 'be moralistic':

> Sometimes a kind of conservative traditionalism drove some of the children to ask me (in the grip of unconscious guilt feelings) for ordinary schooling. I gave it to them willingly. These regressions only lasted ten or so minutes at most.

Some of them protested at his proposals, but the author was 'absolutely firm', saying 'Listen kids, we decided that we can say and do whatever we want here'. Celma recites his *mea culpa*, he lacked the nerve to carry his experiments through to their proper limits:

> I repressed sexual practices when they became too extreme, too exciting. Sometimes I had to hit the kids. I was forced to use my authority when confronted with lies or threatening behaviour. All this was because of fear of legal reprisals. The insufficient radicality of my classes was certainly due to repression, and not to a lack of desire either on my part or on that of the children.

Moreover, this enforced abstinence resulted in great deprivation: 'My physiological constitution has never permitted me to be insensible to caresses, allusions, seductions, feelings; and throughout those weeks the most frustrated person in the classroom was me.' But these experiments, despite the inhibitions, still offered the children the possibility of liberating themselves from an incredible alienation. Next, the children – whom we may

168

no longer refer to as pupils – were asked to describe the
teacher. Sexual allusions were not forthcoming until one
'threw the first bombshell': 'He likes to traffic in women.'
The teacher responded with 'total incomprehension'. The
children modify their statements: 'He likes tickling
women.'

> I refuse this modification –
> 'He likes touching up women.'
> I begin to show a bit of satisfaction when, at ten to
> twelve, a group of girls specify,
> 'He likes touching up women's fannies.'

The children are also encouraged (and how we admire the
so-called neutrality of the author) to reply to the following
questions: ' "What do you think of boys (and girls)?", "If
you were allowed to do whatever you wanted, what would
you do (in a place where there were no parents, no priests,
no schoolteachers, no policemen, and no grownups)?" '.
No doubt the reader understands that those questions,
asked in that kind of context, are bound to produce essentially sexual replies. Sexual themes also appeared in the
drawings that the children were asked to produce. All this
leads Julien Celma to exclaim:

> I was convinced: infantile sexuality exists; and, more
> importantly, exists even during the latency period . . .
> Therefore the idea of a latency period appears as a vast
> smokescreen conjured up by Power, through the inter-
> mediary of its whore: so-called scientific 'objectivity'.
> This is used to account for the real sexual gap which
> usually occurs between the age of five and puberty.
> 'Science' forgets to take into account the repressive

aspect of the social contexts that surround the child. It ignores the reasons for this sexual repression, the sexual 'absence' which, strangely, happens to coincide with the period of family upbringing and of schooling.

Reich, too, contested the universality of the latency period and attributed it to socio-economic factors. The author reassures us that:

> I must emphasize that I never pressured the kids into expressing sexual preoccupations. The fanatics of the 'latency period' always hoped the opposite was true. Because they are afraid; afraid of the revolutionary power of children.

170

Here we can recognize one of Reich's favourite themes, that children and adolescents have great revolutionary potential:

> When an adolescent learns that the suppression of his natural sexual strivings is not due to biological factors, say a death instinct, but rather to definite interests of present-day society; that, further, parents and teachers are only the unconscious executive organs of this social power, then he will not consider this merely a highly interesting scientific thesis, but he will begin to comprehend his misery, will deny its divine origin and begin to rebel against his parents and the powers whom they represent (*Character Analysis*, 295).

The type of sexuality that is manifested by the children thus conditioned (no matter what the author may claim) is basically anal-sadistic, a fact which will not surprise psychoanalysts. A number of things show that the author's idea of sexuality mirrors the level of sexuality of the children who he is 'teaching': 'I was as crude, if not more so than my pupils. I am proud to say that I didn't force myself . . . Many girlfriends benefited from these experiments.'

The author concludes that teachers, and even reformists, are merely 'watchdogs of the system', are simply 'educastrators'. A 'renaissance of love relations without exclusion' has to be built. 'The adult will disappear . . . the revolutionaries will be children, or there won't be any at all' is the thought with which Celma concludes.

We can outline one or two points pertinent to both Reich's and Julien Celma's conception of the latency period. We consider it completely misguided to attribute the coincidence of the 'period of family upbringing and of schooling' and the latency period to the machinations of some 'Power'. Through observation and intuition, educators were led to start children's schooling at five or six – the age at which the Oedipus complex dissolves and when children are particularly psychically apt to benefit from education.

Although he was himself a psychoanalyst, Reich needed reminding, just as much as his feeble follower, that children are not physiologically able to act upon genital wishes. The consequences of human prematurity for hominization itself cannot be overstressed. There is a world of difference between the pregenital sexuality of the child (even when his wishes are genital), and the genital sexuality of an adult. It is because of the father's genital prerogatives that the child chooses him as a model, and wants to grow up to be like him.

The intervention of an adult (often the mother, as in the

case of the perverse masochist that Reich describes in his
clinical material) is harmful to children if that adult col-
ludes in the child's infantile, pregenital sexuality, convincing the child that it has a real equivalent of genital
sexuality. This is the origin of perversion. We no longer
need to grow up, to become like father, because we have
already become an adequate sexual object for an adult.
The sexual games that Celma initiated, like the sexual
promiscuity prescribed by Reich, the discussions,
descriptions, drawings he solicited and all the activities
that excited him, can have the effect of turning these
children into future perverts. The 'educastrator' may
172 have damaged their future lives genitally: the pervert tries
to 'economize' on the castration anxiety that characterizes the genital stage and can only act on pregenital
pleasure, and is thus usually impotent during genital
coitus. He may also have damaged their future relationships, since, being fixated at the pregenital stage, the
pervert has a very restricted and incomplete scope of
object relationships. Paradoxical as it may seem, Reich's
ideas on upbringing will necessarily lead to genital and
orgasmic impotence, and yet this is his criterion for
measuring the full development of human psychosexuality. So Julien Celma has probably been much more of
an 'educastrator' than he realizes.[13] In Julien Celma's
book we found that there was a complete concordance
between two sets of ideas:

1. the 'sexual liberation' of children in the emotional
climate of being seduced by an adult (note Celma's unequivocal insistence on having to push the experiment to
the limit); and

2. the desire for the eradication of adults.

What these two ideas have in common is that they both express a denial of one of the two anchoring points of reality. They work to deny the absolute nature of the difference between the generations. The other difference of similar status is the difference between the sexes; and it is not hard to find many examples of this in contemporary culture.

If the child sees no need to grow up, to identify with the father, in order to be an adequate sexual partner for his oedipal object, or substitute, there is no need for adults to exist as models of maturity. The difference between child and adult is thus reduced to the mere facts of size and age, and there is nothing to prevent the child from being set up as an ideal.

Furthermore, the latency period is thus abolished. We tried to show how latency begins with the dissolution of the Oedipus complex resulting from the child's physiological – genital – inadequacy. The eradication of the 'separation of space for schooling' which the author prescribes comes as the logical conclusion of his premises. To mix up schooling and sexuality, based on the disappearance of the latency period, resulting itself from the disappearance of the difference between the generations, would lead to a real breakdown of culture.

So it is not, in fact, sexual liberation that lies at the heart of this experimentation and these politics, but the eradication of an entire axis of reality. It is an attempt to deny the difference between the generations (the difference between child and adult), and the need for maturation and development, which we find expressed, in a condensed form, in the Oedipus complex.

Even if all these themes are not explicitly contained in

173

Reich's writings, we think that they are, in fact, integral to it and an extension of it, and in some ways they serve to reveal its latent meaning. The disavowal of the Freudian discovery of sexuality, which Reich maintains in order to argue for sexuality in the pre-Freudian sense of the word, leads to this attempt to bridge the impassable gap which separates the child from its parents.

Here we agree with Philip Rieff (1966) when he suggests that the Reichian conception of the child and the adolescent expresses 'his hatred for all the doctrines of maturity, including psychoanalysis'.

CHAPTER VI

REICH'S WORK AND EXOGENEITY

THE CONCEPT OF character armour, one of the major 'discoveries' of Reich's work, spans both the period in which he wrote works that most analysts still find useful[14] (although we have shown that he diverged from Freud from the outset of his work), and the orgonomic period when his latent delusory state of mind became manifest. The dramatic evolution of the theme of the armour, in Reich's work, never fails to strike a chord in anyone, whether a psy-something or not, who is sensitive enough to empathize with the process of a 'descent into hell'.

At first, the armour was a metaphor for the totality of the ego's resistances:

> The totality of the neurotic character traits makes itself felt in the analysis as a compact defence mechanism against our therapeutic endeavours. Analytic exploration of the development of this character 'armour' shows that it also serves a definite economic purpose: on the one hand, it serves as a protection against the

stimuli from the outer world, on the other hand against the inner libidinal strivings (*Character Analysis*, 44).

Fairly soon we see the materialization of the armour. At this point the armour is something which has to be 'loosened'. Next:

> The character consists in a chronic alteration of the ego which one might describe as a rigidity . . . There are 'gaps' in the armour through which libidinal and other interests are put out and pulled back like pseudopodia. The armour, however, is to be thought of as mobile. It operates according to the pleasure-unpleasure principle. In unpleasurable situations the armouring increases, in pleasurable situations it decreases. The degree of character mobility, the ability to open up to a situation or to close up against it, constitutes the difference between the healthy and the neurotic character structure (145–6).

> The armouring may reach such a degree that these gaps are 'too narrow', so that the communication with the outer world is too small to guarantee a normal libido economy and normal social adaptation. A more or less complete armouring is exemplified in the catatonic stupor, a completely insufficient armouring in the structure of the impulsive character. It must be assumed that every lasting conversion of object libido into narcissistic libido results in an intensification and hardening of the armour. The affect-blocked compulsive character has a rigid, unalterable armour which leaves slight possibilities of establishing affective contact with the world; everything bounces back from his smooth hard surface (163).

The superficial layer of the armour, then, consists of aggressive energy . . . the affective block is one great spasm of the ego which makes use of somatic spastic conditions. All muscles of the body, but particularly those of the pelvis and the pelvic floor, of the shoulders and face, are in a state of chronic hypertonia. Hence the 'hard', somewhat masklike physiognomy of compulsive characters, and their physical awkwardness (198).

. . . that sounds logical, particularly when we remember the hardening of the arteries with advancing age . . . What has become solid and immobile hinders life and its cardinal function, the alternation of tension and relaxation, in the gratification of hunger as well as sexual needs . . . *The rigidity renders the rhythm of tension and relaxation impossible.* [Our italics.] Clinical experience shows anxiety to be nothing but the sensation of a constriction (213).

177

One finds that the gap in the armour soon closes up again and the layers of the armour are interlaced (315). . . . In most cases the character attitude of silence is based on a spasm of the throat musculature of which the patient is unaware and which keeps down excitations as soon as they begin to appear (324) . . . The armour can be superficial or deep, soft like a sponge or hard as nails.

Then Reich attempts to demonstrate that 'In character analytic work, we meet the function of the armour also in the form of chronically fixed muscular attitudes. The identity of these functions can be understood only from one principle: the armouring of the periphery of the biopsychic system' (314). He then goes on to postulate 'the functional identity of the character armour and the muscle armour':

> The spasm of the anal sphincter, which leads to a number of severe intestinal conditions, results from an infantile fear of defecation. The explanation that it is due to the pleasure connected with holding back the faeces is incomplete, to say the least. The muscular holding back of faeces is the prototype of repression in general and is its initial step in the anal sphere. In the oral and genital sphere, repression is muscularly repre-sented as a tightening of the mouth, a spasm in the throat and chest, and in a chronic tension in the pelvic musculature . . . These facts show the following: mus-cular rigidity can take the place of a vegetative anxiety reaction, in other words, the same excitation which in the case of fright paralysis retreats to the centre of the organism, forms, in the case of rigidity, a peripheral muscular armour of the organism; (it remains to be seen whether the biological armourings of, say, turtles, develop in a similar manner) (344–7).

178

This observation that emotions, affects and character defences come to be inscribed in our bodies, in posture, is obviously true. We will not challenge Reich's claim that 'word language very often also functions as a defence: the word language obscures the expressive language of the biological core' (362). Those people who practice mas-sage, especially those with psychoanalytical training, would fully agree with this idea. However, what we are trying to uncover is the unconscious fantasy that underlies Reich's theories, unremittingly and to the last of his works. The fantasy that motivates the work right through to its complete transformation into manifest delusion. This is not to say that there are no moments when his theories do correspond to clinical reality. Not everything that issues from the mind of the mentally ill is necessarily madness; madness can in itself contain the partial awareness of a reality which is overlooked by ordinary people, as we have seen. But the fact that a fragment of reality may have been grasped does not invalidate the hypothesis of an underlying delusion.

This point is illustrated, with humour, in the story of Clérambault, a well-known early twentieth-century French alienist who hospitalized the owner of a café. The proprietor was diagnosed as suffering from delusional jealousy. A number of policemen, who regularly frequented both the man's establishment and his wife, were distressed at his internment for a jealousy which seemed to them to be well founded. They wrote to their superior, who spoke to the prefect of police, who wrote to Clérambault. The latter took up his pen and replied, 'If only it had pleased God, Sir, that it was enough to be cuckolded to not be mad.'

The concept of the muscle armour changes once again in Reich's theories when he states that 'the muscle armour has a segmented arrangement' (370).

At the head at least two segmented armourings can be clearly distinguished: one including the forehead, and cheekbone region, the other including lips, chin and throat. A segmental structure of the armour means that it functions in front, at the sides and back, that is like a ring. Let us call the first armour ring the ocular, the

second the oral ring. In the ocular armour segment we
find a contraction and immobilization of all or most
muscles of the eyeball, the lids, the forehead and the
eyelids, empty expression of the eyes or protruding
eyeballs, a masklike expression or immobility on both
sides of the nose. *The eyes look out as from behind a mask.*
[Our italics.] The patient is unable to open his eyes
wide, as if imitating fright. In schizophrenics, as a
result of contracted eyeball muscles, the expression of
the eyes is empty or as if staring into the distance. Many
patients have been unable to cry for many years. In
others the eyes represent a narrow slit. The forehead is
without expression, as if 'flattened out'. Very often
there is myopia, astigmatism, or other visual disturbances . . . The segmental structure of the armouring is
always transverse to the torso, never along it. The only
remarkable exception to this are the arms and legs
(371).

There follows a detailed description of the different seg-
ments of the armour.

From this point onwards, Reich constructs a fantasy
image that he has of his own body. It is covered in a shell
that petrifies him and immobilizes him, as if in a trap. A
strange metamorphosis, strongly reminiscent of Gregor
Samsa's, and which brings to mind the common etymol-
ogy of the words 'segment' and 'insect'. We want to put
forward a hypothesis about the privileged place given to
orgasm, and the role of the armour, in the Reichian system.

First, it is worth recalling that Reich, in the chapter
'The Genital Character and the Neurotic Character', considers the character armour as being of external origin:

180

The character of the ego consists of various elements of the outer world, of prohibitions, instinct inhibitions, and identifications of different kinds. The content of the character armour, then, is of an external, social origin . . . The development from a primitive state to the civilization of today demanded a considerable restriction of libidinal and other gratification. Human development has been characterized by increasing sexual suppression; in particular, the development of patriarchal society went hand in hand with an increasing disruption and restriction on genitality . . . In order to avoid real anxiety (occasioned by actual external dangers) people had to inhibit their impulses: aggression has to be held down even if, as a result of the economic crisis, people are at the point of starvation, and the sexual instinct is shackled by social norms and prejudices. A transgression against the norms means actual danger, such as punishment for 'theft' or infantile masturbation, jail for incest or homosexuality.

181

Here it is worth noting the entirely exogenous nature of the dangers listed by Reich. In Western countries incest or homosexuality incur, at the most, a few months' imprisonment (homosexuality is not usually a crime in itself, and the law only intervenes in the seduction of a minor or indecent behaviour, as is the case with heterosexuality). Is there any comparison between the danger of a few months' imprisonment and the status of the prohibition of incest in the psyche?

Reich continues:

To the extent to which real anxiety is avoided the stasis of the libido and with that the stasis anxiety increases.

Stasis anxiety and real anxiety are in mutual interaction: the more real anxiety is avoided the more intense becomes stasis anxiety, and vice versa. The unafraid individual satisfies his strong libidinal needs even at the risk of social ostracism (163).

The character armour defends the subject against the external world and so protects him from (real) anxiety at the same time as absorbing the anxiety produced by libidinal stasis (libido not discharged through genital orgasm). For the genital character:

182

> Periodic orgastic discharges of libidinal tension reduce the instinctual demands of the id on the ego . . . True, the ego of the genital character also has an armour, but it has the armour at its command, instead of being at its mercy . . . The genital character can be very gay but also intensely angry; he reacts to object loss with depression but does not get lost in it; he is capable of intense love but also of intense hatred (168–9).

And as for the psychic agencies, they all coexist happily:

> The superego of the genital character is sex-affirmative; for this reason there is a high degree of harmony between id and superego. Since the Oedipus complex has lost its cathexis, the counter-cathexis in the superego has become superfluous (167).

In the same chapter the superego is defined as 'a foreign body taken from the threatening and prohibiting outer world'.

Practically speaking, there are no superego prohibitions of a sexual nature. The superego is not sadistic, not only for the reason just mentioned but also because there is no libido stasis to activate sadism. . . . *The ego-ideal and the real ego do not differ greatly from each other; there is, consequently, no appreciable tension between the two* [our italics] (167).

As for the ego:

> The ego takes over, without any guilt feelings, the genital libido and certain pregenital tendencies of the id . . . The ego, as a result of sexual gratification, is under little pressure from the id as well as the superego (168).

183

Here we have the paradise of the psyche, where the lion lies down with the lamb, all thanks to the orgasm. On the other hand, the neurotic is 'incapable of an orgastic liberation of his free-floating, non-sublimated libido'. Overall we cannot overstress the extent to which Reich represents conflict as emanating entirely from the outside world, as we can see in the title of the chapter we discussed earlier: 'A Note on the Basic Conflict between Need and the Outer World' (XIII). For example, in this chapter Reich states that:

> Ambivalence in the sense of coexisting reactions of love and hatred is not biological but a socially conditioned fact . . . Such signs of ambivalence as hesitation and indecision are to be understood as signs of a libidinal striving which urges for expression but which again and again is inhibited by fear of punishment (284).

The first antithesis between sexual excitation and anx-

iety is only the intrapsychic reflection of the basic
antithesis between individual and outside world
(286).

The chapter ends with these claims:

> Thus, the hypothesis of the death instinct makes one
> forget completely that the 'inner mechanisms' which
> constitute an antithesis to sexuality are moral inhibi-
> tions which represent the prohibitions imposed by the
> outer world, by society . . . It remains to be shown that
> the 'unmastered destructive impulses' to which human
> suffering is ascribed are not of the inhibition of sexuality
> by authoritarian education which makes aggression a
> power beyond mastery, because inhibited sexual
> energy turns into destructive energy. Those aspects of
> our cultural life which look like self destruction, finally
> are not the manifestation of any 'impulses to self
> destruction', but the expression of very real destructive
> intentions on the part of an authoritarian society inter-
> ested in the suppression of sexuality (290).

184

So, in Reich's theory, the character and muscular armour
represent the bodily inscription of external prohibitions
which are of social origin. A diagram (373) shows that 'the
direction of the orgonotic streaming is transverse to the
armour rings', and this stream moves by virtue of undulatory contractions. The diagram and commentary are
unmistakably reminiscent of the peristaltic movement of
the intestines. Reich comments: 'The segmental structure
of the muscular armour represents the worm in man . . .
It is biological energy itself which moves in these wave-
like movements' (374). In *The Function of the Orgasm* (276),

Reich again compares the contractions to the movements
of a 'worm' or to the 'peristaltic movement of the intestines'. The inadequate relaxation of the armour is given
the following comment (in capitals in the text): 'As SOON
AS THE EXPRESSION OF GIVING MEETS ARMOUR
BLOCKS SO THAT IT CANNOT FREELY DEVELOP, IT
CHANGES INTO DESTRUCTIVE RAGE' (375). Taken as a
whole, these descriptions suggest some problem on the
level of sphincter control. We think it possible that the
idea of a character (and muscular) armour, which is of
external origin, represents a common persecution fantasy.
The fantasy of being constricted and immobilized in the
rectum of the persecutor, who prevents the subject from
moving. This fantasy is activated during the period of
toilet-training, because the parent who conducts the
training seems to control the child's (anal) discharge by
making it dependent upon his goodwill, as if the child
were locked into the sphincter of his 'trainer'.

185

We have found Reich's concept of orgasm to be simply
an equivalent of an anal discharge, which is experienced
as a triumph over the trainer-persecutor, whose constraints the subject has managed to conquer. The armour-
rectum is also the equivalent of a projection of a regressive
and restrictive superego (Reich describes the armour as a
kind of law that we are 'at the mercy of' – see above).

In reality, orgasm, in itself, has no particular value or
merit in our view. True, it is a discharge of tension, and
this is inherently a kind of evacuation (Alexander writes of
'drainage'), but the tension in question is of a more complex nature than the purely anal. When orgasm is seen as
representing a victory over some enemy it is wrong to give
it the significance of the highest developmental stage in

psychosexual maturity, and to place it at the centre of a
theory of genitality.

We have identified the concept of armour with the
persecution fantasy of being caught in a trap, which is the
equivalent of the rectum; there are many examples of this
fantasy to be found. In fact, every confined space from
which it is impossible to escape – castles, fortresses,
islands, prisons, concentration camps – can take on this
meaning in the unconscious. Places are always identified
with parts of the body in the unconscious. The settings of
Edgar Allan Poe stories (dungeons and death chambers),
the Sadean scenarios, all contain a number of elements
that could be characterized as anal symbolism. Rudolf
Hess, the Auschwitz *Gauleiter*, called the camp 'the anus of
the world'. To be trapped inside the anus of the other, or
trapping the other in one's own anus, these are the positions between which the subject oscillates. The victim of
such a persecution will eventually become the persecutor.
This interpretation of the character armour, in Reich's
work, we feel to be confirmed in the light of what he wrote
in *The Function of the Orgasm* (1942), in Chapter VII called
'The Function of a Living Bladder'. The body is compared to a taut bladder: 'Patients complain of being tense
to the point of bursting, filled to the point of exploding'
(258).

> Bearing this picture of an armoured bladder in mind,
> let us imagine a biopsychic organism whose energy
> discharge is impaired. The surface membrane would be
> the character armour . . . The biological energy urges
> toward the outside, whether to seek contact with people

186

and things or to seek pleasurable discharge. Thus, this urge to expand corresponds to the direction outward from within. The surrounding wall of the armour counteracts this urge. The armour not only prevents the bursting, it exerts a pressure from the outside towards the inside. Rigidification of the organism is its ultimate effect . . . The patient feels himself tense to the point of bursting but it is as if he were tied down (261–2) . . . If indeed one were to exert and maintain continuous pressure over the entire surface, that is, prevent it from expanding in spite of continuous inner production of energy, it would be in a perpetual state of anxiety; that is to say it would feel constricted and confined (279).   *187*

It is worth remembering that the metaphors of bursting and of explosion are, typically, linked to the anal-sadistic phase. The fantasy that underlies the entire theory of the biology of orgone, and the function of the orgasm, is, as in all cases of psychosis, close to consciousness by virtue of being in a deformed state. In this case we have been displaced from one sphincter to another.

So, we have seen that the discharge of energy, in orgasm, is equivalent to an anal evacuation which the external world (society, parents, educators) as embodied in the 'armour', is trying to obstruct. But why is it that orgasm is so necessary, if it is the expulsion of the libido, the life energy? We saw earlier that Reich considers 'sexual stasis' to be the cause of many illnesses; and that he considers that the damming up of the libido produces a resexualization of past objects and past forms of satisfaction. In fact, it is hard to find a theory of psychosexuality that is more normative and prescriptive than Reich's; his study of the 'genital character' (quoted above) is a masterpiece of prescription. Beneath the so-called 'sexual revolution' there lies an intolerant puritanism.[15] He writes: 'the perverse or neurotic forms of satisfaction from which society should be protected are in themselves only substitutes for genital satisfaction and only appear when genital satisfaction is impaired or made impossible'.

When Reich begins to investigate orgone, vegetative current, and bioelectricity, he paints an impressive picture of the psychic and somatic problems that can arise from any impairment of orgasmic discharge. This includes cancer, ulcers, rheumatism, circulatory problems, emphysema, etc. It is as if the stasis (which is, of course, of entirely social origin) 'poisons' the mental and bodily organs. Remember also that Reich was later to discover DOR, the orgonic death energy, the antithesis of orgone or life energy:

188

> There is a deadly orgone energy. It is in the atmosphere. You can demonstrate it on devices such as the Geiger counter. It is a swampy quality. You know what swamps are? Stagnant, deadly water which doesn't flow, doesn't metabolize. Cancer too is due to a stagnation. Cancer is due to a stagnation of the flow of life energy in the organism (1952, 89–90).

Now, this rather grandiose, delusional fantasy has an ordinary and commonplace prototype: if you don't defecate you will end up poisoning yourself. This fantasy may account for some mothers' manic supervision of their children's excretory functions. However, the life energy stagnating in the body, which ends up being identified

with poisonous excreta, seems, at least at the outset and in
Reich's orgonomic period, to have been identified with
beneficial properties. In fact, cosmic orgone energy is
nothing less than God himself: 'I simply affirm having
discovered, in a practical utilizable form, a "natural fact",
marked by a series of characteristics which up until now
were attributed to "God" or "Ether"' (1949).

Note that, from the moment that Reich finds God, he
abandons his earlier forms of projection. The roots of
human suffering are now far more grandiose, although no
less exogenous:

> I began to err when I held religion alone responsible for
> human suffering. I did not know that the error of
> religion was a symptom, not the cause, of human bi-
> opathy. I persisted in the error when I held the personal
> interests of a social group – parents or educators –
> responsible for suppressing human love life. I did not
> know that the suppression of love life is no more than a
> mechanism, and by no means the final cause, let alone
> intention, of certain social circles.
>
> When I was under the spell of the great socialist
> movement and worked for years as a physician among
> the underprivileged strata of the people, I fell into the
> gross error of thinking that 'the capitalist was respon-
> sible for the human plight'. It took the brutal experi-
> ence of the deteriorating Russian Revolution to free me
> from this error. They had killed the capitalists, but
> misery continued to grow; diplomatic intrigues, pol-
> itical manoeuvring, spying and informing on others, all
> of which they had set out to eradicate, were more
> powerfully at work than ever . . . For years and in

189

harmony with Freud's doctrine, I committed the error of thinking that the unconscious was 'evil' and 'responsible for all misery' . . . Whether or not I am falling into a new error, I do not know. I assume that it is correct to trace human distress to the pathology of human structure, which in turn lies in its armouring, and to hold the armouring responsible for the orgastic impotence of the human animal, but all this may be a mere mechanism. . . . It probably lies in the relation of the human being to the cosmic energy that governs him (*God, Ether and the Devil*, 46–47).

190   The case of President Schreber may help us understand the evolution of Reich's delusions (*S.E.*, *12*). At the heart of all paranoia, says Freud, there lies a fantasy of passive homosexuality which cannot be accepted by the ego, as it feels extremely threatening. President Schreber, at the start of his illness, struggles with a delusion dominated by persecution fantasies. Over time these ideas change, he is promised a great destiny, he will be transformed into a woman as part of a divine plan. God will impregnate him, with his divine rays, and the President will give birth to a new race of men. Schreber's sexual desires become acceptable to his narcissism by being displaced on to God; the persecutory paranoia becomes a mystical delusion. Thus President Schreber is reconciled to his passive homosexuality, and so obtains a 'sort of cure', says Freud.

Despite being more obscure (and more systematized), Reich's delusions seem to develop along similar lines to Schreber's. Some of the signs we have already noted, others include his pathological jealousy, his disgust at homosexuals, and his megalomania. Reich claimed: 'I simply laid my eagle's egg in a hen's nest', referring to the 'nest' of Freudian psychoanalysis; here the image of the eagle laying an egg is a condensation of both his mega-lomania and his feminine identification.

At the heart of Reich's psychosis we also find a wish for passive submission, against which he ardently defends himself. Because this wish is narcissistically unaccept-able, he experiences the outside world (family, pa-triarchal society, educators, capitalism, etc.) as persecutors. Then, as he feels himself united with the cosmic energy of orgone, of Ether, of God, the persecution dies away. Now the armour becomes the obstacle between the self and the union with God, the fusion with the cosmos:

> Since, in the unarmoured organism, every plasmatic current and orgonotic excitation, in reaching for con-tact, runs into a wall, an irrepressible urge develops to break through the wall no matter what the circum-stances or means. In so doing, all life impulses are converted into destructive rage. The organism tries to break through the armour by force, as if it were imprisoned.
>
> I seriously believe that in the rigid, chronic armour-ing of the human animal we have found the answer to the question of his enormous destructive hatred and his mechanistic-mystical thinking. We have discovered the realm of the devil (119).

But now that the character armour can no longer be blamed on religion, society, parents, educators or the unconscious, what is it? Reich answers: 'There must be a reason for not being united with "God"; there must be a way to unite again, to come home' (121).

The armour that separates man from God the Father is now seen as the work of the devil (remember that Reich identifies himself with the Son of God in his book *The Murder of Christ*): 'The devil is an essential function of the armoured animal, man' (124). At this point an entirely new concept appears – the fear of orgasm: 'The core of the matter is the deep anxiety in the organism, so-called orgasm anxiety, which keeps man from realizing himself and his aspirations. We know that it is the armouring of the human animal that threw it off the path of rational biosocial living' (132).

192   We are in the middle of a circular argument: the 'orgasm anxiety' comes from the armour and the armour comes from 'orgasm anxiety'. It is as if Reich, having discovered God, can now let go of part of his secondary revision and part of his manic rationalization; from this point onwards his projections take place on a cosmic scale with God as *ultima ratio*. At one level, union with God and orgasm have been confused: 'Orgasm anxiety is to a simple neurotic anxiety reaction as a flood that inundates millions of acres of farmland and takes thousands of human lives is to a break in a water pipe in our home' (133). Once again, we find the hydraulic metaphor, but this time on an apocalyptic scale; the dam has burst and the tidal wave threatens.

When an individual whose armour is breaking down in overall fashion is left to himself, suicide, murder or psychotic breakdown is the most likely outcome. It is the sudden loss of control over the deep forces of the bio-system that constitutes the danger. It is furthermore, or rather first of all, the incapacity of the organism to deal

with the full force of the natural bio-energy that makes
the situation in such cases so dangerous . . . In addition, the healthy individual whose bio-energy is discharged regularly in the genital embrace never develops the amount of energy stasis that would add the
surging impact of pent-up emotions to the danger of the
breakdown of the armour.

To summarize: the incapacity of the armoured bio-
system to cope at all with strong bio-energy, the great
amount of dammed up energy due to lifelong stasis . . .
constitute the danger (133–4).

This new theme of 'orgasm anxiety', the fear of losing
control, may throw some light on the fantasies underlying   *193*
Reich's work. We remember Ilse Ollendorf's descriptions
of his fear of thunderstorms, gales and natural forces, and
bear in mind that the result of overwhelming anxiety is a
sort of psychic death. Then turning to the third part of the
trilogy, the Ether, Reich writes:

In order to make God a living reality, the armouring
must be destroyed and the identity of God and primal
life, of devil and distorted life, firmly and practically
established. Unfortunately, God and life process,
which is nowhere so clearly expressed as in the orgastic
discharge, are identical. Once this approach to God
was blocked, only the devil could reign (138).

Reich considers Ether to be cosmic orgonic energy, and,
ultimately, God: 'the orgonotic current in man, or,
expressed differently, "the flow of ether" in man's mem-
branous structure. For many ages, religion has called this
primal force "God"'(159).

On closer examination, this orgonotic current/primal force/God appears to have certain characteristics which confirm our interpretation of the Reichian delusion: 'Orgone energy can be demonstrated everywhere. Accordingly it *penetrates* everything, though at varying rates of speed' [our italics] (142). We find: 'a charging from the surrounding orgone ocean, and an energy discharge in the surrounding energy ocean' (144).

The other characteristics of orgone energy include its undulatory and pulsating movement, and its visibility in the dark ('Autogenous lumination'): 'when the observer's organism has stimulated the orgone of the room to a sufficient extent . . . rapid, yellowish-white lightning-like streaks of light (*Strichstrahlen*) cross the room in all directions' (152). Also: 'the organism's orgone energy apparently excites the atmospheric orgone energy and vice-versa'; orgone energy 'emits' or 'develops' light (153), produces heat (154), or static electricity (155). Orgone can be concentrated in orgone chambers or in orgone accumulators. Extended exposure of patients to the accumulated orgone allows them to 'recharge themselves' (156).

We feel that all these details furnish us with enough information to formulate an interpretation of what Reich's developing delusion both reveals and conceals. This orgonotic current, which penetrates us and which we must discharge during orgasm (or else fall fatally ill), is actually a penis. The concept of the 'energetic penis' has been described by analysts (Nunberg, 1948; Grunberger, 1954) as an introjection of the penis of the father, or some strong and admired substitute, which the subject experiences as a 'beneficent' re-energizing. This is a variation of the mechanism of identification.

194

VI]   REICH'S WORK AND EXOGENEITY

The fantasy of being penetrated by the father's penis can be found from the earliest of Reich's works, initially in the form of his concept of 'libido' or 'sexual energy'. Yet as this is unacceptable to the ego, it cannot be retained within the body, and so becomes dangerous. It has to be evacuated as quickly as possible at the risk of various 'biopathies'. Such a fear can also be found when analysing hypochondriacs, where we often find the unconscious fantasy of having incorporated an object (the breast or penis) which then threatens to destroy them, or to damage their vital organs. For these people, as for Reich, sexual excitation may be experienced as a bad internal object which must be got rid of at all costs. Sometimes, an *195* overactive genital life or over-frequent masturbation may be a sign of this inability to bear accumulating excitement.

We remember Reich's theory that a healthy individual never has large quantities of energy to discharge; such defensive splitting of genital energy into smaller units has been studied by Ferenczi (1924).

It seems as if the author of *The Function of the Orgasm* experiences, in the violence of orgasm and the resulting loss of control, a fantasy of being mercilessly surrendered to an object who is both loved and hated, desired and feared. The ego is threatened with annihilation by the invasion of the object and the excitement it calls forth. The concept of 'orgone energy' is a condensation of both object and drive, and hearkens back to the earliest days of life, when 'outside world, object and impulse are identical' ('Instincts and their Vicissitudes').

Sometimes a mystical paranoia may relapse back into its earlier persecutory form, which cannot be entirely

contained within the religious delusion; such as in the case
of Schreber. We can see aspects of both these stages of
paranoia in Reich's partial reconciliation with a body
which has been transfixed by divine orgonotic energy.
This representation of a homosexual reunion with the
father staves off the need to project all 'evil' on to
patriarchal society (or its homologue, capitalism). It
could be said that Reich, after a long struggle, has managed to 'unite again, to return, to come home', as he put it.

It is important to draw out the parallel development of
Reich's paranoia and his thought as this can throw some
light on his political theories. We cannot overstress the
196   continuity between what is known as Reich's 'European'
period and his 'American ' period. We hope that we have
demonstrated that what is conventionally thought of as a
theoretical rupture is, in fact, only a change of form produced by the transformations inherent in paranoia. The
paranoia was present at the beginning, in latently delusional ideas (sexual energy and the function of orgasm), and
eventually became manifest. Its manifestation in religious
ideas reflects a fairly common psychotic process; we find it
in Strindberg, as well as Schreber and others. The twin
poles of Reich's paranoia are the hatred of patriarchal
society, and the love of God. Everywhere we encounter
the problem of the father.

We might be criticized (as well as being criticized for
being unrepentant 'Oedipalists', which is to say – psychoanalysts) for having analysed someone, although the
analysis is by no means exhaustive, through the inter-
mediary of his writings, and thus not in the analytic
setting. We could reply, to such a criticism, that in the first
place psychotics find it impossible to tolerate the analytic

setting (Ilse Ollendorf notes this in the case of Reich)
which obliges us to find other forms of investigation; and
secondly, Freud likewise analysed the most famous of all
paranoiacs in psychoanalytic and psychiatric literature,
Schreber, through his writings.

Everywhere, we are brought back to the problem of the
father, and yet beneath this wish for a grand reunion with
God the Father we find another fantasy. You will probably have guessed already, the fantasy is that of a dissolution into the cosmos, a fusion with the primary object – the
mother, a desire to return to the time when the ego was not
separated from its ideal by a painful and irreparable split.

197

CHAPTER VII

THE INTERNAL CONTRADICTIONS OF FREUDO-MARXISM

IT IS REICH's book *The Mass Psychology of Fascism* (1933) that could, properly speaking, be called Freudo-Marxist. We want to explore the contradictions to be found in such theory, both in relation to psychoanalysis and to Marxism. Although our interest is primarily with its contradictory position *vis-à-vis* psychoanalysis, there is another contradiction that exists, both explicitly and implicitly, in the relation Reich's work has to Marx.

We are not being critical of the attempt to construct a psychoanalytic theory of Fascism. We have tried to show how the essence of Freud's theories relates to a wide scope of extra-therapeutic applications of psychoanalysis. We have also listed a number of Freud's works in which he describes psychoanalysis as part of the analysis of society and culture. It is a shame that he never tried to analyse the Nazi and Fascist phenomena, when he did give us his analysis of religion and, briefly, Marxism. Perhaps the fact that Reich wrote his 340-page book on Fascism, using

his own theory, served to discourage Freud from undertaking this task. Freud's energy was already dwindling
and this project would have meant fighting a battle on two
fronts: on the one hand, against Fascism; and, on the
other hand, against the Reichian application of psychoanalysis to the explanation of Fascism.

But since Marxist analysis of Fascism and Nazism,[16] in
terms of economic factors alone, is so pitifully inadequate,
the urgent need for another explanation is completely
understandable. So, in our eyes, Reich's attempt is fully
justified. We are only going to criticize his theories in so
far as they result from his anti-Freudian stance.

Reich returns to his ideas of *Character Analysis* and his   *199*
concept of a double layer of unconscious drives. The first
(which is located beneath the secondary, superficial layer
– consisting of apparently polite and honest attitudes
etc.):

> consists exclusively of cruel, sadistic, lascivious,
> rapacious and envious impulses. It represents the
> Freudian 'unconscious' or 'what is repressed'; to put it
> in the language of sex-economy, it represents the sum
> total of all the so-called 'secondary drives'. The Freud-
> ian unconscious can be comprehended as a secondary
> result of the repression of primary biologic urges . . . If
> one penetrates through this second layer of perversion,
> deeper into the biologic substratum of the human ani-
> mal, one always discovers the third, deepest layer,
> which we call the biologic core. In this core, under
> favourable social conditions, man is essentially an
> honest, industrious, cooperative, loving and, if moti-
> vated, rationally hating animal (1933, xi).[17]

It is clear that Reich considers man to be naturally good-
natured, unless social conditions make him otherwise.

> Yet it is not at all possible to bring about a loosening of
> the character structure of present-day man by penetrat-
> ing to this deepest and so promising layer without first
> eliminating the non-genuine, spuriously social surface.
> Drop the mask of cultivation, and it is not natural
> sociality that prevails at first but only the perverse,
> sadistic character layer. It is this unfortunate struc-
> turalization that is responsible for the fact that every
> natural, social or libidinous impulse that wants to
> spring into action from the biologic core has to pass
> through the layer of secondary perverse drives and is
> thereby distorted. [This idea of a natural social instinct
> of biological origin is extremely doubtful.] This distor-
> tion transforms the original social nature of the natural
> impulses and makes it perverse (xii).

Next comes the description of a concept that is blatantly
contradictory. It sums up the fundamental contradiction
between Marxism and Freudianism, and makes all
Freudo-Marxist enterprises seem doomed to failure, from
the point of view of conceptual coherence. Reich suggests
transposing 'human structure into the social and political
sphere', and continues:

> It is not difficult to see that the various political and
> ideological groupings of human society correspond to
> the various layers of the structure of the human
> character. We, however, decline to accept the error of
> idealist philosophy, namely that this human structure
> is immutable to all eternity. *After social conditions and*

changes have transformed man's original biologic demands and
made them a part of his character structure, the latter reproduces
the social structure of society in the form of ideologies (xii).

The first sentence, which considers ideologies to be a
reflection of the human character structure, is in keeping
with a psychoanalytic theory of the relations between
individual and society. The second sentence, on the contingent nature of this structure, is a concession to Marxism;
a concession which the third sentence (italicized by Reich)
reinforces ('the character structure reproduces the social
structure of society in the form of ideologies') to the point of
totally inverting the first proposition. The first and last
sentences of this 'statement' are to one another as Freudianism is to Marxism: they are saying the same thing as long
as one is inverted in relation to the other.

According to Reich, Fascism is representative of the
second layer of the character; 'Fascism is nothing but the
organized political expression of the structure of the aver-
age human character, a structure that is confined neither
to certain races, nor nations, nor political parties, but is
general and international'. This proposition is completely
unacceptable to a Marxist since it makes no reference to
the forces and relations of production. 'My character-
analytic experiences have convinced me that there is not a
single individual who does not bear the elements of
Fascist feeling and thinking in his structure. As a political
movement Fascism differs from other reactionary parties
inasmuch as it is borne and championed by masses of
people' (xiii–xiv). This statement, that Marxists would
reject because of its generality, would be acceptable to
psychoanalysts if, in fact, this 'single individual' was not

201

someone who simply had the misfortune to be born into a
patriarchal society, as the rest of the book goes on to
argue. Reich takes up the theme of the descent of the
patriarchal family, 'fallen' from the Golden Age of
maternal rule. Elsewhere he claims that the patriarchal
family is the 'motor force' of the authoritarian structure of
the state:

202

> In the figure of the father the authoritarian state has its
> representative in the family, so that the family becomes
> its most important instrument of power. The
> authoritarian position of the father reflects his political
> role and discloses the relation of the family to the
> authoritarian state. Within the family the father holds
> the same position that his boss holds towards him in the
> production process. And he reproduces his subservient
> attitude towards authority in his children, particularly
> in his sons. Lower middle class man's passive and
> servile attitude towards the Führer-figure issues from
> these conditions (53).

Fascism exploited this behaviour:

> This is not a question of an 'inherent disposition', but of
> a typical example of the reproduction of an
> authoritarian social system in the structures of its mem-
> bers. What this position of the father actually necessi-
> tates is the strictest sexual suppression of the women
> and children (53).

In these extracts from Reich's book we can easily see the
radical difference from Freudian analysis; psychoanalysis
interprets the representation of psychic structures as
reflected in society. Sexual repression is of preponderantly

endogenous origin, which external repression can, at most, confirm.

But in our opinion, Marxists will be no more satisfied with Reich's analyses than are psychoanalysts. His descriptions of the historical conditions in which Fascism is located lack elements that are essential for a dialectical analysis. The place given to the father and the family throws doubt on the very concept of class. If Reich is talking about the 'middle class' here it is difficult to see how he intends to differentiate it from the proletarian family and father. Is not the proletarian father even more subjugated to his 'superiors'?

Furthermore, the mother is given exactly the same   *203* treatment; the author notes many references to maternal imagery in National Socialist mythology, and comes to some conclusions:

> What is important in this connection is that the tie to the authoritarian family is established by means of sexual inhibition; that it is the original biological tie of the child to the mother and also of the mother to the child that forms the barricade to sexual reality and leads to an indissoluble sexual fixation and an incapacity to enter into other relations.

Here Reich has a footnote:

> Hence the Oedipus complex which Freud discovered, is not so much a cause as it is a result of the sexual restrictions imposed on the child by society. Yet wholly unconscious of what they are doing, the parents carry out the intentions of authoritarian society.

And the text continues:

> The tie to the mother is the basis of all family ties. In
> their subjective emotional core the notions of homeland
> and nation are the notions of mother and family . . .
> Thus nationalistic sentiments are the direct con-
> tinuation of the family tie and are likewise rooted in the
> fixated tie to the mother. This cannot be explained
> biologically. For this tie to the mother, in so far as it
> develops into a familial and nationalistic tie, is itself a
> social product (57).

204

The reader may already have guessed the next stage of the
argument: patriarchal society ('political reaction's germ
cell' and 'the most important centre for the production of
reactionary men and women' (104–5)) hampers the
healthy individual's sexual economy, thus impeding liberation. The impediment derives 'from a nostalgia for an
unsatisfied orgasm'. From this issues the mysticism, the
'unconscious nostalgia for orgasm'; from which comes the
masses' appetite for Fascism, which is 'the supreme
expression of religious mysticism'. The logic is dualistic,
we have a universal evil – sexual stasis, which is responsible for cancer, schizophrenia and Fascism; and, its
obverse in a universal panacea – orgasm.

To try to understand Fascism as a form of mysticism
was a perfectly valid aim for Reich. And his concern to go
beyond a Marxist economic analysis was also perfectly
justified. He seemed to try to reconcile his hypotheses
with Marxist theory by proposing to study 'the role of
ideology and the emotional attitude of the masses as a
historical factor, a question of the repercussion of the
ideology on the economic basis' (10). He is critical of :

> vulgar Marxism [which] completely separates econ-

omic existence from social existence as a whole, and
states that man's 'ideology' and 'consciousness' are
solely and directly determined by his economic existence. Thus it sets up a mechanical antithesis between
economy and ideology, between 'structure' and 'superstructure'; it makes ideology rigidly and one-sidedly
dependent upon economy, and fails to see the depen-
dency of economic development upon that of ideology.
For this reason the problem of the so-called 'repercussion of ideology' does not exist for it. Notwithstanding
the fact that vulgar Marxism now speaks of the 'lagging
behind of the subjective factor' as Lenin understood it,
it can do nothing about it in a practical way, for its
former conception of ideology was too rigid. It did not
explore the contradictions of economy and ideology,
and it did not comprehend ideology as a historical force
(14).

Reich could also have referred to 'The Eighteenth
Brumaire of Napoleon Bonaparte', where Marx vividly
evokes the stranglehold of the past upon the living; it
returns as 'spirits of the past' which come to possess the
living: 'The tradition of all the dead generations weighs
like a nightmare on the brain of the living.' For Reich it is
ideology itself that must be considered as a material force,
as is suggested in his title for the first chapter of the book,
'Ideology as a Material Force'.

In as much as a social ideology changes man's psychic
structure it has not only reproduced itself in man but,
what is more significant, has become an active force, a
material power in man who in turn has become con-

cretely changed, and, as a consequence thereof, acts in a different and contradictory fashion (18).

It is, of course, the concept of 'psychology of character analysis' that guides us through this spectrum, from the authoritarian family to the problems of sexual economy it produces.

We feel that although Reich invented a system, which he was perfectly entitled to do, he was nevertheless wrong to use Freud and Marx as reference points for his system. It may be useful to quote a well-known passage from the 'Theses on Feuerbach' in *The German Ideology* (1845):

206   The production of ideas, of conceptions, of consciousness, is at first directly interwoven with the material activity and the material intercourse of men – the language of real life. Conceiving, thinking, the mental intercourse of men at this stage still appear as the direct efflux of their material behaviour. The same applies to mental production as expressed in the language of politics, laws, morality, religion, metaphysics, etc. of a people. Men are the producers of their conceptions, ideas, etc. That is, real, active men, as they are conditioned by a definite development of their productive forces and of the intercourse corresponding to these, up to its furthest forms. [Next comes the famous metaphor of the *camera obscura*.]

. . . we do not start out from what men say, imagine, or conceive, nor from men as narrated, thought of, imagined, conceived, in order to arrive at men in the flesh; but set out from real active men, and on the basis of

VII]   INTERNAL CONTRADICTIONS

their real life-process demonstrating the development
of the ideological reflexes and echoes of this life-process.
The phantoms formed in the brains of men are also
necessarily sublimates of their material life-process . . .
Morality, religion, metaphysics and all the rest of ideology as well as the forms of consciousness corresponding
to these, thus no longer retain the semblance of inde-
pendence. They have no history, no development; but
men, developing their material production and their
material intercourse, alter, along with this, their actual
world, also their thinking and the products of their
thinking. It is not consciousness that determines life but
life that determines consciousness (*Collected Works*, Vol.   *207*
5, 36–7).

Whether one agrees with these views or not, they are at
the heart of Marxism. They have been taken up in subsequent Marxist works, For example, Engels writes,
'Dialectical philosophy itself is nothing more than the
mere reflection of this process (material life-process) in
the thinking brain' (1888, 240).

Psychoanalytic theory, without being in the least idealist, considers that primary drives – aggressivity and the
hunger for love – determine the economic conditions
themselves. This theory tends to see social institutions as
the exosmosis of the unconscious, a projection of the
drives and the defences against the drives. Such a theory
gives a place to the human unconscious, as the basis of
social institutions, which accounts for the specificity of
psychoanalytic analyses of social and political phenomena (which is obvious, even tautological), and which

also accounts for the resistances which this kind of work inevitably encounters.

When political systems, and other sociopolitical institutions, are reduced to their unconscious roots, there follows a loss of a defence, which may feel indispensable to an apparent autonomy. Political ideologies are attempts to interpret political facts, to decode social reality, and these attempts invariably move in the opposite direction to psychoanalysis, which looks for the unconscious determinants, the instinctual bases, of these facts. The aim of political ideologies seems to be to ascribe the source of human suffering to external factors. This usually entails blaming a system (private property, capitalism, patriarchy, the 'consumer society'), or a group of people (Jews, the bourgeoisie, 'armoured characters', *homo normalis*, or oedipalists), or even society in general, for human suffering. Ideologies never seek to explain these miseries as the effect of the drives, or of the human condition itself, but they try, instead, to escape this suffering. And this, no doubt, is their main function. Furthermore, they extend the promise of a reconciliation between man and his lost unity; be it Marx's 'complete man', or the purified Aryan race, the non-armoured genital character enjoying his full orgasmic capacity, or the neo-Rousseauist return to nature. All these ideologies are based on a denial of castration: a castration which psychoanalysis stresses and which religions deny.

Political ideologies are excellent examples of projective systems, seeing the causes of human misery in external factors. Remember that projection results from the ego's tendency to expel from it anything which causes unpleasure (mainly the internal excitations and the drives), and to thus make an exclusively pleasure-seeking 'purified' ego. Freud calls this the 'purified pleasure-ego', and it functions to contrast itself with an 'outside' world which is strange and threatening. To use Freud's words, 'the ego has severed a part from itself which it projects into the outside world, and which it experiences as hostile'. The economy of the psyche is such that it is not, in fact, possible to escape the pressure exerted by the drives; and if these are 'projected' into the outside world they are invariably re-experienced as persecuting. Once expelled, the drives will return towards the ego in order to be reintegrated into the space from which they were expelled, that is, the ego itself.

Ideologies and their interpretations of social and political facts are thus, to varying extents, paranoid formations. When their founder or originator is also found to be in the grip of a persecution fantasy, as was the case with Rousseau for example, this structure is all the clearer to see. The idea of man as being born to be 'good' is a representation of the 'purified pleasure-ego'; in order to be rid of his 'bad' drives these are projected on to 'external' forms such as the social organization or private property. Yet whatever part of itself the ego has detached and expelled will be bound to pursue the subject and persecute him. We have given a similar interpretation of Reich's persecutory projections, and his persistent faith in human nature as 'naturally' honest and amiable, but alienated by character armour, patriarchal family structure and authoritarian society for a start. Hitler's racist theories are, of course, almost caricatures of this mechanism: the projection of evil on to the Jews, who were then experienced as persecuting and who had, therefore, to be destroyed. This form of behaviour is pathognomic to paranoia and its persecutor-persecuted oscillation.

It is much more difficult to 'interpret' Marxism because it is scientific in its method. However, its system of analysis is also projective, compared to psychoanalysis, because only the latter is based on a theory of the primacy of internal factors. Marcusian theories, like all ultralefts to some extent, are an interpretation of sociopolitical facts which is particularly projective and persecuting. We will note only one of the statements from Marcuse's book *One-Dimensional Man*; the one-dimensional man is the person who lives in a society of abundance. This society has managed to make the needs of the individual correspond exactly to the needs of the society by creating false needs, via the mass media and especially by advertising. These false needs are aimed at increasing consumption, thus creating a process of production which demands 'the need for soul-destroying work which is not really necessary', says Marcuse. It is not the individual who is the source of his needs, as his needs are imposed on him from the outside, by society. The ensemble of social controls is 'internalized', and in fact individuals are seen as so completely invaded by social laws that there is no 'private space' which would allow them any critical distance from which to dissent from the system.

Individuals identify themselves with the existence imposed on them . . . and find satisfaction and fulfilment in it. This identification is not an illusion, it is a reality. However, this reality is only a more advanced stage of alienation, it has become completely objective, the alienated subject is absorbed in his alienated exist-

VII]   INTERNAL CONTRADICTIONS

ence, there is only one dimension: it is everywhere and in all forms.

Marcuse also writes of a 'conditioning, which fashions the aims and instinctual drives of the individual'. In our opinion, these few sentences show, almost to the point of caricature, what we have been trying to point out about the fundamentally projective and paranoic essence of ideological analyses. The concept of 'false' needs is diametrically opposed to psychoanalysis. In the latter, every psychic manifestation, every form of human behaviour, has deep infantile roots and is related, although sometimes at great distance, to the primary drives. It would be impossible for a society to create needs if these did not have some internal meaning – corresponding to some unsatisfied infantile wish. But Marcuse completely inverts the problem by positing a 'conditioning, which fashions the aims and instinctual drives of the individual', drives which, according to Freud, are intangible and ahistorical. In Marcuse's view it is the 'outside' (industrial society) that has invaded the inside (the ego and the drives), a process which mirrors the persecution fantasy at its height. Finally, for Marcuse, outside and inside come to coincide. Not because man projects himself outwards, basing his behaviour and actions on his internal psychic model; but because the outside (the 'system', social organization, etc.), like a veritable *deus ex machina* has come to appropriate the individual's ego, who thus becomes 'possessed'.

These explanatory models of political ideologies are very much like the 'influencing machine' fantasy that is so characteristic of paranoid-schizophrenics, which has

211

been brilliantly described and analysed by Tausk (1919). Many paranoid-schizophrenics believe themselves to be under the influence of a machine which is operated by enemies who control their bodies, genital organs and minds by exerting various currents or waves on them. The subjects feel that certain of their ideas are being inflicted on them, are foreign to them, are coming from outside. Tausk discovered that the 'influencing machine' is nothing but the projection of the subject's own body. The patient, unable to accept his drives and wishes, tries to rid himself of them in the form of an imaginary machine. The economy of the psyche is such that when the body is projected, in the form of a machine, there is a tendency for it to become persecutory, feeling like an invasion of the patient's 'purified' ego.

212

To summarize our argument, then: because political ideologies analyse sociopolitical facts in terms of a projective, and sometimes persecutory, system of interpretation, they tend to disconnect these facts from their unconscious roots. This disconnection opposes the reconnection that psychoanalysis tends to make. The latter connects disparate human activities and systems, understanding these as projections of the drives and their defences. We have mentioned two kinds of projection, and these should not be confused. This second kind is a consequence of the fact that human beings can only act, and create, on the basis of their internal, psychosexual, model. We project this model out on to the world when creating political systems, institutions and economic structures, thus making them in our own image. In other words, this kind of projection is a translation of psychic space into social space. In the case of the political analysis of these systems, the first kind of projection, this entails a defence against acknowledging the connections between the human psyche and its creations. The result is that the creations seem to escape from their creators, becoming independent creatures, omnipotent Golem, which invade from the outer world and mould the human psyche.

Another aspect of political ideologies that we noted is their tendency to foster the illusion of the possibility of escaping from castration. This characteristic of political ideologies is very much linked with their projective aspect. Once it is purged of evil, be it represented in the form of the Jews, private property, capitalism, patriarchal society, character and muscular armour, or any other projected object, the purified ego can exist without conflict, man can be united with God. In *Aden Arabie*, Paul Nizan says: 'When man shall be whole and free he will no longer dream at night'. In other words he believes that there will come a time when all desires will be fulfilled. Psychoanalysis, however, maintains that human incompleteness, and thus human desire, will never disappear. Humanity is destined to dream from here to eternity.

At the heart of all ideologies lies the romantic and fashionable idea of 'changing the world'. Psychoanalytic understanding tends to act against this idea. By returning the creation (economic systems, social institutions, sociopolitical facts) to the creator (the human psyche) it burdens man with an unbearable responsibility and guilt. We not only have to bear the burden of acknowledging, and taking responsibility for, the drives we have tried to expel but we also have to tolerate having our narcissism undermined, since psychoanalysis dispels Illusion. 'We call a

213

belief an illusion when a wish-fulfilment is a prominent factor in its motivation, and in doing so we disregard its relations to reality, just as the illusion itself sets no store by verification' (Freud, 1927, *S.E.*, *16*, 31).

If social reality actually stems from its roots in infantile conflicts, primary drives and their defences, man cannot hope to 'change the world' or to regain wholeness, because these primary drives constitute an unchangeable, undeniable, undialectical core. The psychoanalytic vision of the world is not optimistic; human nature can only be changed within certain limits. War will not disappear, and as we have said, paradise will never be regained. Both Illusion and illusions must be mourned.

This does not mean that change is impossible, for the Oedipus complex and the narcissism resulting from prematurity push mankind to surpass his limits and press forward. But the primary drives cannot be 'surpassed', so a revolutionary overthrow of the relations of production for example, which would close off some of the drives' outlets would lead to these same drives being discharged via other outlets. This is why such revolution is impossible and accounts for processes such as the birth of a 'new class',[18] and other ways in which 'the return of the repressed' will occur.

In short, then, psychoanalysis confronts man with his own drives, deprives him of the outlet of projection, and makes him give up certain hopes. So psychoanalytic interpretation is diametrically opposed to ideological interpretation. People who are in desperate need of the illusion of a better, brighter tomorrow and who thus need the defences that political ideologies offer will, understandably, be most opposed to psychoanalytic interpretation of sociopolitical facts. That is why it is easier to switch ideologies than to give up all ideology, as is borne out by general observation. Apart from a few exceptions which are linked to specific changes in an individual economy, it is easier to switch from Fascism to Maoism than to move from Trotskyism to political indifference. Another exception to this is that the switch may be from politics to religion or to drugs. Examples of this general rule include Paul Nizan the writer, who switched from Fascism to Communism, Drieu, who switched the other way around, Doriot, the French Fascist leader, who had previously been a well-known Communist, amongst many others.

Max Weber commented that science tends to produce a disenchantment with the world. Psychoanalytic interpretation also produces such a disenchantment, especially in political matters and especially at a time when politics occupies a place that was once occupied by religion. For we should remember that the Freudian project is, above all, a process of reason which aims to use knowledge to illuminate entire areas of psychic life which would otherwise remain obscure. Freud wrote, in 1932; 'Our best hope for the future is that intellect – the scientific spirit, reason – may in the process of time establish a dictatorship in the mental life of man' (*S.E.*, *21*, 171). And in this respect, Reich's work seems like a moment of the irruption of the irrational within psychoanalysis, and – in some respects – within Marxism too. It is also an attempt, no doubt unconscious, to destroy both these systems. Since each of these systems claims to be scientifically consistent, and yet their respective projects are so different and even diametrically opposed, any attempt to synthesize them will only produce an explosive mixture

215

which will destroy both. Here it might be possible to hazard an interpretation of such an attempt at synthesizing Freud and Marx. Bearing in mind that Freudo-Marxists claim to take 'Marx as mother and Freud as a father', such a synthesis would represent a fantasy of a sadistic primal scene resulting in the destruction of both parents.[19]

Michel Clouscard, author of an invigorating pamphlet: 'Néofascisme et Idéologie du Désir' (1973), is critical of Freudo-Marxism on precisely these grounds. He mainly focuses on *Anti-Oedipus*, which he considers to be 'the latest step . . . towards a neo-fascist anthropology'. Clouscard thinks that works such as this are an attack on the old bourgeoisie, on behalf of the new middle classes, in order to destroy it and usurp its power, so Freudo-Marxism becomes an instrument of war. We leave the author the responsibility for his hypothesis but take the following quote from his book:

216

> This syncretism is an anti-epistemological ideological operation, it works by:
> 1. removing from Freud and Marx their fundamental epistemological discoveries;
> 2. taking up the Freudian and Marxist corpus (now amputated of their essence) as a common discourse.
> 3. This common discourse constitutes a pre-Kantianism (is pre-critical), it is not a discourse of metaphysics (because before science metaphysics had a value and had its dignity) but actually constitutes an antiscience.

In our opinion all attempts at Freudo-Marxism entail the destruction of the original core of each of the two systems. In fact, it would come as no surprise if this turned out to be the aim of many of the Freudo-Marxisms that abound today . . . Science (like the Oedipus complex) is the expression of reality. As such it is unwelcome to those who desire the 'great decoded flows', and who cannot wait to have their apocalyptic desires fulfilled. Before a different kind of apocalypse, in 1932, Gide wanted, in the name of Communism, 'to be on the same side as those who made Socrates drink hemlock'. But he had the courage to change his mind after visiting Soviet Russia.

To understand the return of Reich today we should take a tip from *The Mass Psychology of Fascism* and look for the connections that exist between his mythology and the public that is welcoming him back. Perhaps we could also consider Freud's description of his own feelings when observing Michelangelo's Moses, ready to destroy the Tables of the Law in his anger at the idolators unable to resist the spell of Illusion:

> How often I have . . . essayed to support the angry scorn of the hero's glance! Sometimes I have crept cautiously out of the half-gloom of the interior as though I myself belonged to the mob upon whom his eye is turned – the mob which can hold fast no conviction, which has neither faith nor patience, and which rejoices when it has regained its illusory idols (*S.E.*, *13*, 213).

EPILOGUE

THE MURDER OF REALITY

No more waiting
We're erect
We're ready for the revolution
It's happening now.
We must act *now*
Because we are living now.
Paradise Now.

(*Paradise Now*, Julian Beck, *On 1*, mimeographed publication.)

218   **S**INCE WE FINISHED writing this book many things have occurred to confirm our suspicions that the 'return to Reich' signals a growing tendency to recreate Illusion. We have heard three papers on Reich (read by E. Kestemberg, R. Angelergues and R. Cahn) expressing views which correspond with our own.

In February 1974, Payot published the first French language translation of Reich's *The Cosmic Superimposition*, the sequel to *God, Ether and the Devil*. In the book we can clearly see Reich's fantasy of a primal scene, which has grown to cosmic proportions. Yet despite the explicit nature of this fantasy Reich continued to maintain that his work constituted a 'scientific discovery' and backed this belief up with diagrams, illustrations and reports of sightings. Here is a glimpse of this delusional cosmology:

> Inert mass is being created by superimposition of two or more spinning spiralling orgone energy units through loss of kinetic energy and sharp bending of the elongated path toward circular motion. [Followed by a

diagram called 'The creation of the primordial mass particle (m) through orgonotic superimposition', showing two corkscrews joined at the tip to form a helicoid structure.] A functional relation is hereby established between the spinning movement of mass-free orgone energy (OR) and inert mass (m), which also characterizes the relationship of heavenly bodies spinning in the surrounding orgone ocean. Spheres or discs of solid matter spin on a spiralling path within a faster-moving wavy orgone energy ocean, as balls roll forward on a faster-moving, progressing water wave . . . Furthermore, [this discovery] makes comprehensible the fact that our sun, and our planets move in the same plane and in the same direction, held together in space as a cohesive group of spinning bodies. The spinning wave is the integration of the circular and forward motion of the planets, of their simultaneous rotation on the N–S axis and their movement forward in space. The orgone ocean appears as the primordial mover of the heavenly bodies (187).

And so on . . . for one hundred and eighty pages . . .

All right. Since, thank God, we do not have censorship, everyone is free to write, publish and read whatever they choose. But when a French university academic is interviewed on television in a programme on Fascism and is asked to comment on people who claim that W.R. was mad at the end of his life, and replies, 'It's quite simple: to say that Reich was mad – that's Fascism' . . . it makes you wonder.

First, one wonders whether the academic believes in a conspiracy of physicists, biologists, doctors, astronomers, chemists and physiologists who are ganging up against 'Reichian discoveries', which have not been recognized by science (let us repeat this one last time, just in case anyone is still unsure). If the academic does believe in these 'discoveries', he ought to bring the matter to the attention of academic authorities of the world, so that justice can be done to Reich's work. Then all the scientists, living or dead, starting with Einstein, who responded to Reich's work with a wall of silence may be denounced. Reich's later works, remember, claimed to be part of the natural sciences. It is clear that, whereas the social sciences, psychology, history and other humanities, can be endlessly disputed, a 'scientific' theory as part of the 'hard' sciences is, given the resources available these days, taken up or dropped relatively quickly.

220

If, on the other hand, our academic does not believe in the Reichian discoveries, we might be allowed to suppose that his education has provided him with some intellectual skills which he would do well to use in this case. We might expect him to wonder, for example, why it is that a man spends twenty-odd years of his life in laboratories, conducting experiments which are all patently false. Why he devotes an extraordinary amount of energy to describing these experiments, and publishes them in innumerable volumes (after Freud, Reich is probably the most 'prolific' analyst), in which he claims to have found the cure for all human suffering and, ultimately, to have found the secret of life itself. Even if our academic had no contact with psychiatrists or psychoanalysts around him, who could inform him of the precise nature of the illness which these symptoms indicate, he should be able to come to the conclusion for himself that there is something rather strange about such behaviour.

But our academic does not follow any of the courses we envisaged. So we have to assume that our alternatives (that either he believes or he does not) are false, and that the solution lies elsewhere. The only other possibility is that he just does not recognize our point of view and simply refuses to put the problem in our terms – 'Don't trouble me with facts'. Since for him, as for many others, the work of W.R. fulfils a function, its rationality is of little importance, or, more likely, must remain unquestioned. This corresponds to our definition of Illusion; a belief motivated by wish-fulfilment requiring no confirmation from reality. Here we find, on the intellectual level, a kind of paradox described by Kierkegaard on the ethical level: we cannot choose between good and evil, but can only choose the possibility of choosing, that is, between being moral or amoral. We might want to look, these days, for the equivalent of 'anomie' on the level of mental functioning. Moreover, psychiatry classifies 'moral insanity' as a psychic disturbance, thus demonstrating that, frequently, logical and ethical reasoning is based on a distorted view of reality.

221

As for the Fascists, a term which is used so glibly these days, we can now see what is meant by the term: the Fascists are those people who destroy the Illusion, and the Führer of the Fascists is called 'Reason'.

We have claimed that the present fad for W.R. typifies a trend. It may well be temporary, but others of a similar nature will take its place. We have stressed the way in which he fragments both Freudianism and Marxism, since both these theories claim to be scientific. We would also like to stress that if Reich's later work (which the majority of even his most devoted sycophants have rejected) is now to become part of ultraleft (and academic) thinking, this must be for the simple reason that it coincides with a fundamental and contemporary wish. Such a wish might be likened to Nietzsche's aspiration to a 'cosmic sensibility'. It is well worth reading Jean Brun's beautiful and profound book, *Le Retour de Dionysos* (1969), on this subject:

> Dionysus promises the expansion of the ego as far as the boundaries of the world and the transcendence of the narrow corporeal prison in which every man is jailed, by letting him taste the ecstasy of an infinite life. Thus, Dionysus, master of time and space, is the Evangelist of a cosmic sensibility . . . Nietzsche enables us to predict a renaissance which will terminate the age of punitive God, for it will put an end to the curse of individuation. But while waiting for the reconstitution of Dionysus' fragmented body he searches all the fields of nature for something that will be an organic ocean, to bring together his scattered members in an act of identification, at the heart of the ocean, submerged in a great wave of being, in an immense cosmic shudder.

So it is not important that Reich's orgonotic theories are insane. It is, in fact, impossible for them not to be, as they are the reflection of a deep psychotic regression, one which casts the subject back to the threshold of life itself, and, before that, to his prenatal life. It is a regression to what Federn, in *Ego Psychology and the Psychoses* (1952), describes as the 'egocosmic self', which exists before the differentiation between ego and non-ego. The significant

222

thing is that such theories express the human urge to merge into the All-encompassing, and to transcend the ego. Jean Brun, quite correctly, links Eros to Dionysus, but it is a Platonic Eros: 'Eros is essentially a disembodiment. To be otherwise would be impossible since Eros is, above all, an escape from this world and a transcendence towards that "up above" where man can identify with God'.

Neither the 'sexual revolution' of today, nor that already described in Reich's work, has anything to do with Freud's discovery of the importance of sexuality. Reich, and his 'anti-oedipal' heirs, do not see sexual practices as being in any way related to the integration of the drives, or even to pleasure itself. They bring us 'beyond the pleasure principle', in what amounts to an attempt to get rid of the distance between desire and satisfaction, the difference which, according to Freud, constitutes the incentive which presses us forward 'forever unsubdued' (1920, S.E., 16, 42). But this discrepancy between desire and satisfaction is inherent in the human condition. It rests mainly on the insatiable oedipal incestual desire which, at the oedipal age, the child is incapable of satisfying, and which makes all our love objects into substitutes for the original object. Only a return to primary fusion could close the distance which separates desire from its complete satisfaction, and which separates the ego from its Ideal. Sexual 'liberation' or 'revolution' is actually in essence narcissistic, and being so can be classified as Illusion.

Freudian psychoanalysis cannot and does not hold out the promise of removing the split which is fundamental to the human condition. It simply aims at allowing people the happiness that is possible, given the limits imposed on

223

us by our specific prematurity. These limits include our dependence on our objects, the Oedipus complex, and the differentiation of the agencies of the psychical apparatus (the ego and superego as derivations of the id) – in short, the rather limited channels through which desire must pass if it is to be satisfied, instead of the 'great decoded flows' of anti-oedipal fantasy.

Today, following a period of uncritical worship, Freud is the object of violent attacks from the intelligentsia. This is probably because people who wanted to plunge into the abyss of the unconscious, or who wanted a 'sexual liberation' to break free from restrictions, thought that Freudian theory offered such a possibility. These people rapidly encountered the constraints of the human condition, which psychoanalysis tries to define rather than transcend. The illusion was destroyed and the author trampled underfoot, like a primitive idol which has failed to give satisfaction.

We have repeatedly stressed, in other writings, the attempts that are made in our culture to do away with the difference between the generations. There are equally powerful attempts to deny the difference between the sexes. These two differences are indissolubly linked. We witness the latter in the 'unisex' style certainly, but also in the transvestism and transsexualism that seem to be flourishing in the streets and in films, theatre and music.

Délirante Sarah was a montage of several scenes narrating the life of Sarah Bernhardt. It starred a man in drag, wearing extravagant dresses dripping with rhinestones and pearls, as Sarah; whilst women dressed as men played the male roles. It was a baroque and fascinating spectacle, as was *Axel* (after Villiers de l'Isle-Adam), a film by Rosa von Praunheim, who is a man (although his name does not necessarily convey the fact). The heroine is played by a transsexual. The first act takes place in a convent. The part of a nun is played by a male transvestite, the bishop is played by a woman. Thus, the heroine calls the man '*meine Mutter*' and the woman '*mein Vater*'. These West German film-makers are currently making many films starring transsexuals, which have a strange and poisonous charm. Among these are the films of Schröter, Fassbinder, and also of D. Schmid, who, although he is Swiss, belongs to this school of film-making. It goes without saying that, as individuals, every transvestite and transsexual may well be caught up in distressing emotional conflicts; but what interests us in this phenomenon is, firstly, its extent and, secondly, the fascination which it exerts. It seems to act out the fantasy that 'anything goes'. We can also recall the sinister hero of *A Clockwork Orange*, the film by Stanley Kubrick, whose sexual ambiguity is expressed in his face, in the disturbing asymmetry of the eyes, one of which is painted with exaggeratedly false eyelashes.

225

Jean Brun has described our fascination with the 'monstrous' as embodying the dissolution of the ego, which is both the stuff of dreams and of nightmares. He recalls the *Temptation of Saint Antony*, with its swarming mass of monsters, his transmigration of all corporal forms. It is noteworthy that, in the heretics' scene, the characters are travestied in the clothes of the opposite sex; the prototype of the monster is actually the hermaphrodite. This is because being both man and woman, he escapes the most fundamental form of human destiny, sexual identity. (Our term sex comes from the Latin *secare*, indicating a scission or split.) If the double difference of the generations and of the sexes constitutes the intangible heart of reality, what we are witnessing is a contemporary attempt to murder that reality.

In the relatively recent past we have noticed a similar attempt at effacing this double difference, in two of the main films about the rise of Nazi Germany. Bob Fosse's *Cabaret* opens in Berlin, 1931. The film opens with a transvestite dance number presented by the *compère*, a strange and disquieting character, like a male doll, with make-up and high-pitched voice, who leads the dance, like Satan in Gounod's *Faust*, the dance of the cabaret and who represents *Hitler in uns*. The scenes of the transvestite cabaret punctuate the entire film and we see reflected in this microcosm, as under a magnifying glass, the successive stages of the Nazis' unstoppable rise to power.

226

Visconti's *The Damned* introduces us very quickly into the same world. The hero dresses up as Marlene Dietrich in *The Blue Angel*, and shows himself like this to his reunited family. By raping a young girl (in an identification with Stavroguine which is not gratuitous) and committing incest with his mother, he erases the difference between the generations. The element of perversion which is to be found in these two films, which are in some ways mere catalogues of sexual deviation, in itself indicates the desire to eliminate the double difference which is characteristic of perversion. Concentration camps and Nazism, however, cannot be explained away as merely a matter of sexual perversion, in the way that Liliana Cavani attempts in *The Night Porter*. The pervert's attempt to murder reality is only a breach through which will surge an entire cortege of split-off destructive drives. The pervert opens only the doors of the night.

In perversion the superego, heir to the Oedipus complex and thus responsible for reality-testing, is cast off, and the destructive drives are freed. The prohibition of incest implies that the mother belongs to the father; it also carries the message that the son, at the oedipal age, does not have the capacity to fulfil the mother and consequently that the father possesses prerogatives not shared by the son.

Jean Brun has understood that the counterpart of Dionysus is the Grand Inquisitor. The murder of reality inevitably leads to violence and anomie. In *The Devils* (or *The Possessed*), a title which must have inspired Visconti, we find not only the story of the rape of the young girl, but also the gradual instigation of total amorality. Note that the 'Devils' are nihilists (they are, in fact, the 'Popular Vengeance' group led by Nechaev):

227

Listen, I've summed them all up: the teacher who laughs with the children at their God and at their cradle is ours already. The barrister who defends an educated murderer by pleading that, being more mentally developed than his victims, he could not help murdering for money, is already one of us. Schoolboys who kill a peasant for the sake of a thrill are ours. The juries who acquit all criminals without distinction are ours. A public prosecutor, who trembles in court because he is not sufficiently progressive, is ours, ours. Administrators, authors – oh, there are lots and lots of us, and they don't know it themselves. On the other hand, the docility of schoolboys and fools has reached the highest pitch; the schoolmasters are full of bile; everywhere we see vanity reaching inordinate proportions, enormous

bestial appetites . . . Do you realize how many converts we shall make by trite and ready-made ideas?
When I went abroad, Littré's theory that crime is
insanity was the vogue; when I returned, crime was no
longer insanity, but just commonsense, indeed almost a
duty and, at any rate, a noble protest (Dostoyevsky,
1871, 421).

Attempts to murder reality, then, extend to both reason
and ethics. Man finds himself 'Beyond Good and Evil'
when he tries to transgress the limits of reality constituted
by the double difference. As long as Freudian psychoanalysis may be believed, temporarily, to be a means of
making Illusion into reality, it will still be rejected, at the
first opportunity, in favour of whatever kind of mysticism
or dissident form of psychoanalysis presents itself. On
closer examination, the dissidents can all be seen to shore
up Illusion. Moreover, in times when Illusion is activated
by the social context, some analysts, whose professional
motivation is primarily narcissistic, are prepared to give
up psychoanalysis in favour of whatever ideology seems to
promise them satisfaction; or, what is worse, they will
distort psychoanalysis to make it consistent with the
ideology in question.

In this vein, we recently attended an alarming event
which was organized by a group of analysts who call
themselves 'Freudian'. Actively participating were a
number of members of 'official' psychoanalytic societies
who cannot (yet) express themselves in a like manner
within their own associations. Among other case histories,
we had described to us that of a guerilla who had become
unable to participate in armed combat following a situ-

ation in which he had had to kill a man. The analysis, which took place in 'a Third World' country, was being paid for by the revolutionary organization of which he was a member. The case was not being described by the analyst himself but by a 'French colleague'. After a while, the guerilla had said that he realized his motive for being a fighter was that he wanted to kill his father (and, in the transference, the analyst), and that he could no longer see any point in returning to war. The analyst then 'understood' that this was a 'defence', and that the patient was using analysis as a 'refuge' from the reality of class struggle. He told this to the patient, who then had a dream which 'confirmed' what the analyst had 'understood': lying on a comfortable couch he was awakened, but instead of the alarm clock he could hear the chant 'Comrade, the Revolution calls!'. End of story. Exit the patient, reborn as a guerilla fighter.

229

At no time during the presentation did either the audience or the clinician giving the report raise any questions about the professional ethics that arise in such a case, when the fighter's analysis was being paid for by his organization. Were the parties warned about the uncertainty of the outcome of the treatment, as regards the guerilla's ultimate choice (to re-enlist or to give up combat)? Instead, the guerilla's reticence was unhesitatingly and immediately considered to be an inhibition – albeit an inhibition about killing – and that remained the definition of the problem. The guerilla's murder-mechanism was malfunctioning, and it was brought to the analyst to be put right. The analytic material is not even worth mentioning, as it was only present as an alibi. It seems as if everyone forgot one tiny detail: that when a dream presents a *manifest* content it is the analyst's job to uncover its *latent* meaning. Now there is no way that 'Comrade, the Revolution calls!' can have the unconscious meaning of 'Comrade, the Revolution calls!'; it does not necessarily mean the reverse, but simply put, the unconscious meaning will be something else.

The colleague describing the case history thought that the analyst was projecting on to the patient his own wish to be a guerilla fighter. But this was said without a hint of criticism. Quite the opposite, nobody seemed to feel that it might be somewhat cynical to send a patient away to kill and be killed, while the analyst remained comfortably seated in his armchair, with his good 'revolutionary' conscience assuaged. The event took place beneath the panelled ceilings of a seventeenth-century château. The report was made with an Idi-Amin-Dada joviality, which gave the event the atmosphere of a hallucination. The colleague finished his report by stating, to a completely unruffled audience: '*Il s'agit de savoir à qui ça sert*'. (It's a question of knowing who benefits.)

In other words, this kind of analysis is no longer attempting to uncover the truth of a situation, but places itself at the disposal of 'the Cause'. The moral and intellectual fraudulence of this project were not called into question; the damage done to the human being by this kind of treatment, and the reduction of psychoanalysis to a form of brainwashing were ignored. Nobody questioned the absolutely totalitarian nature of the statement 'It's a question of knowing who benefits', which echoes statements such as Hitler's 'Whatever serves the cause of Germany is right.' And the reader may be able to guess who were labelled as Fascists when these questions were finally raised.[20]

When Freud lamented the fact that (in America) psychoanalysis was becoming the 'housemaid' of psychiatry, he had no idea that it would later become the 'housemaid' of the Revolution; and what a revolution . . .

Because of the sexual, cosmic and political themes in the various periods of Reich's work, it prefigures the unlimited, but rather imprecise, goals described by the high priests of Illusion. Because of this, whatever setbacks it may encounter, it is destined to return to popularity over and over again. It makes happy all those people who would take Freud's well-known maxim, expressing the goal of the analytic process,

WO ES WAR, SOLL ICH WERDEN,[21]

and dream of replacing it with:

WO ICH WAR, SOLL ES WERDEN.

231

NOTES

232   1. This was the situation in France at the time when the book was being written; that is, in 1975.

2. American psychoanalysis has seemed, for these last few years, to be coming out of its period of 'splendid isolation'. There has been a great interest in European work. We hope that it will allow the training of lay analysts.

3. Freud often (and especially in *Civilization and its Discontents*) stressed the asocial nature of love and lovers. Despite the fact that 'group marriage' is usually undertaken as a stance against society and for the 'freedom' of the individual, the deeply anti-individualistic ideology of such an institution is revealed whenever couple-love is criticized for being 'egotistic'.

4. The first edition of *Character Analysis* was published in January 1933 and comprises the first two parts of the second, 1948 version. It contains works from the years 1927–1933.

5. Freud had begun to recognize the structure of the family romance in paranoia. This can be seen in *The Origins of Psychoanalysis: Letters to Fliess*, 47.

6. The translation of the title does not reflect the parallel between Reich's title and Freud's *Massenpsychologie und Ich-Analyse* (1921), which was translated as *Group Psychology and the*

Analysis of the Ego. Reich's book might be more accurately rendered as 'The Group Psychology of Fascism'.

7. By performing some rather alarming mental gymnastics, another Freudo-Marxist, Marcuse, affirms the existence of the death instinct; and goes on to accuse those analysts who do not believe in it of 'revisionism'.

8. We are not aiming to make an exhaustive study of Reich's work, nor to give complete summaries of those works we do discuss. We have already mentioned some books that perform this task quite well. We want to mention a book that has just been published as we are writing ours: Luigi de Marchi's *Wilhelm Reich – Biographie d'une Idée* (1973). This well-documented book is notable for being a political critique of Reich's work, which nonetheless considers his 'orgonomic period' as being the apex of his theory. The author states: 'I should make it clear, straight away, that I consider this period of Reich's work far from the delusional madness that his critics accuse him of. It is this period that shows his best ideas and most brilliant insights.' And since, as we mentioned earlier, Einstein did not agree with Reich's 'discoveries', de Marchi claims that: 'the great physicist made no great contributions to either the science or ethics'. Our own aim is simply to bring together some of the elements in Reich's work which seem to constitute a negation or disavowal of Freud's 'psychoanalytic revolution'.

9. According to many ethnologists it is extremely unlikely that there ever existed any matriarchal societies such as were hypothesized by Bachofen. In our view, his hypothesis rests on a kind of psychological truth, even though it was proved socially inaccurate. It represents a fantasy which reflects the successive phases of a child's development by projecting them on to mankind in general. The child's first experiences are of being entirely subjected to maternal authority. The father then takes over this authority. ('All the power lies with the bearded ones', Molière.) The child needs to escape from the hold of the archaic imago of the omnipotent mother, and the figure of the father is

233

of help in the child's bid for freedom. It could be supposed that patriarchal social organization corresponds to this process which is so crucial to the individual's development. Too intense a fear of the primal mother can lead to an exaggeration of the bond with the father. This will be an obstacle to a positive oedipal relation to the mother from being established. Such a defence may prevail in authoritarian patriarchal societies which allow no space to women. In the extreme, these societies could be thought of as homosexual; women there are relegated to the status of objects. It is no accident that these same cultures created the institutions of the harem and of extended homosexuality.

10. In other words, the situation of 'having' many women represents an inversion of the original oedipal situation, the woman being placed in the position of the child *vis-à-vis* his 'unfaithful' mother, who had several love objects.

11. We apologize to the authors of *Anti-Oedipus* for employing a term which is so redolent of 'familialism'. ['Affiliation' shares a Latin root with 'fils', son.] The term came to us spontaneously. Language is, no doubt, one of the first things to succumb to the 'oedipal degeneracy' that Deleuze & Guattari denounce so vigorously.

12. The book's effect can be seen, for example, in this statement quoted in an opinion poll conducted by *France-Soir*, 'Mariage à la Française', 26–27 September 1971: 'We want to live for ourselves, with friends to entrust ourselves to all kinds of people', said Françoise and Jean. 'Then we will have children. They will be dirtier than other children, but they'll be better equipped for living, above all they won't be educastrated.'

13. At the end of J. Celma's book there is a collection of letters from readers, mostly from teachers who display very sound common sense. To challenge these, Celma prints the letters of support that were written to him when he received a court summons. He was eventually sentenced to two months' imprisonment, with a suspended sentence and approximately £100 fine. His support included letters, written to the court,

from: M. M. Pagès, Maître de Recherches at the CNRS, Dr Chambron, Maître-assistant at the Faculté des Lettres et Sciences Humaines de Toulouse, and a Member of the Society for Psychoanalytic Research in the French Language (a person we do not have the honour of knowing), and, no surprise, Gilles Deleuze; all of whom found great promise in Celma's educational experiments. Meanwhile the Parti Socialiste Unifié of the town in which Celma had 'worked' distributed a pamphlet which was not particularly critical of his 'experiments'. When he returned, two years later, to the class with whom his experiments had produced the best results, Julien was dismayed to find that most of the children had completely 'forgotten' about their strange adventure. Nobody can say for sure what the outcome will be of this process of repression.

235

14. We agree with the importance of Reich's emphasis on analysing resistances, especially in certain states of mind, and we consider some aspects of his technique to be valuable. However, it is impossible to be too careful regarding the possible consequences of emphasizing defence mechanisms. Once again, this may be done at the expense of a consideration of unconscious contents. Reich's statement that:

> The most important theoretical question . . . is the question as to the structure, function and genesis of the ego from which defence stems; for our therapeutic work will be efficient to the extent to which we understand ego defence. If our therapeutic abilities are to be extended it is no longer by a better understanding of the id but of the ego (*Character Analysis*, 304)

prefigures, it seems, 'ego psychology'. There is a tendency, in one American school, to reduce all psychoanalysis to ego psychology; this tendency to reduction is countered by all schools in the European psychoanalytic movement.

15. Also in this line of thought, Reich's preface to *The Invasion of Compulsory Sex Morality* notes with approval that in Russia a Soviet citizen can be taken to court for pinching a woman's bottom or her cheek.

16. Note that Reich, like many people, conflates Fascism and

Nazism. He is actually writing about German Nazism. We should also note, in passing, that Fascism is not based on antisemitism, although many Fascists become antisemites. In one chapter, 'Le Nouveau Racisme', of his book *L'Univers contestationnaire* (1969) André Stéphane considers the relation between the ideas of the New Left and those of the French Fascist pre-war writers; he also looks at the ways in which Fascism may exist in revolutionary movements even though 'objectively' speaking, Fascism was serving the interests of capitalism – or rather, used capitalism to serve its own ends. A new book, *L'Illusion fasciste* (Allaistair, 1973), subtitled 'Fascism and the Intellectuals 1919–1945', stresses the fact that: 'for Fascists, Communism and Fascism were parallel paths. Not only were Fascists convinced that their movement was revolutionary, but they were also convinced that it was leftist' (11).

236

17. Reich altered the vocabulary of *The Mass Psychology of Fascism* when he changed his mind about Communism. Some of these alterations are explained in the preface, but it is not always possible to identify such changes in the body of the text. Unfortunately, we were unable to obtain a first (German) edition of the book.

18. Milovan Djilas, *The New Class: an Analysis of the Communist System* (1957).

19. Remember that W.R.'s mother committed suicide after he denounced her to his father, and that his father, in despair, managed to catch a fatal illness.

20. Jean Brun notes from a book by C. Andler, *Nietzsche, sa Vie et sa Pensée* (1958), on the Dionysian revels in which young men and women came down the hillsides in spring, to dance in the fields, intoxicated with the festival spirit, and concludes: 'Whoever met them was either seized by the same contagious frenzy, or was abused by them like an unrepentant sinner before God.'

21. 'Where id was, there ego shall be.' (*The Ego and the Id*, 1923). The psychoanalytic process is clearly described as being the ego's conquest of territories that were once governed by the

id. The forms of contemporary culture we described above are an attempt to invert this process; to do away with the ego, which puts limits on the field of possibilities. 'Where ego was, there id shall be' could be the motto of those who champion the cause of complete instinctual freedom, those who worship the absence of boundaries, and the high priests of schizo-analysis. This motto is already implied in the work of Wilhelm Reich.

BIBLIOGRAPHY

(The abbreviation *S.E.* denotes *The Complete Psychological Works of Sigmund Freud* (24 volumes), Hogarth Press, London, 1953–74. In the following list, the place of publication is London, unless otherwise stated.)

238   Allaistair, (1973) *L'Illusion fasciste*. Paris: Gallimard.

Andler, C. (1958) *Nietzsche, sa Vie et sa Pensée*. Paris: Gallimard.

Besançon, A. (1960) 'Vers une Histoire psychanalytique', *Les Annales*, nos. 3–4, Paris.

Boadella, D. (1972) *Wilhelm Reich: the Evolution of his Work*.

—— ed. (1976) *In the Wake of Reich*. New York: Ashley Books, 1978.

Brun, J. (1969) *Le Retour de Dionysos*. Paris: Desclée.

Celma, J. (1971) *Journal d'un Éducastreur*. (Symptôme 2.) Paris: Champ Libre.

Chasseguet-Smirgel, J. (1971) 'Les Résistances aux Applications extra-thérapeutiques de l'Analyse, ou la Présence d'une Illusion', in *Pour une Psychanalyse de l'Art et de la Créativité*. Paris: Payot. Also in *Psychanalyse et Sociologie*. Éditions de l'Université de Bruxelles.

—— (1973) *The Ego Ideal*. Free Association Books, 1985.

Clouscard, M. (1973) 'Néofascisme et Idéologie du Désir', in *Les Tartuffes de la Révolution*. Paris: Denoël.

Deleuze, G. & Guattari, F. (1972) *Anti-Oedipus: Capitalism and Schizophrenia*. New York: Viking Press, 1977.

Djilas, M. (1957) *The New Class: an Analysis of the Communist System*. New York: Holt.

Dostoyevsky, F. (1871) *The Devils*. Harmondsworth: Penguin Books, 1971.

Eissler, K. (1965) *Medical Orthodoxy and the Future of Psychoanalysis*. New York: International Universities Press.

Engels, F. (1888) 'Ludwig Feuerbach and the End of Classical German Philosophy', *Marx-Engels Collected Works*, Vol. 5. Lawrence & Wishart, 1976.

—— (1893) 'Letter to Franz Mehring, 14 July 1893', in *Marx and Engels: Basic Writings on Politics and Philosophy*, ed. L. Feuer. Fontana, 1969.

Federn, P. (1952) *Ego Psychology and Psychoses*. New York: Basic Books.

Ferenczi, S. (1913) 'The Ontogenesis of Symbols' and 'Stages in the Development of the Sense of Reality', in *First Contributions to Psychoanalysis*. Hogarth Press, 1952.

—— (1920) 'Further Development of an Active Therapy in Psychoanalysis', in *Further Contributions to the Theory and Technique of Psychoanalysis*. Hogarth Press, 1926.

—— (1924) *Thalassa: A Theory of Genitality*. Albany, N.Y.: Psychoanalytic Quarterly, Inc., 1938.

Freud, S. (1894) 'On the Grounds for Detaching a Particular Syndrome from Neurasthenia under the Description "Anxiety Neurosis"', *S.E.*, *3*, 87.

—— (1895) 'Project for a Scientific Psychology', *S.E.*, *1*, 283.

—— (1898) 'Sexuality in the Aetiology of the Neuroses', *S.E.*, *3*, 261.

—— (1900) *The Interpretation of Dreams*, *S.E.*, *4–5*.

—— (1901) *The Psychopathology of Everyday Life*, *S.E.*, *6*.

—— (1905) *Jokes and their Relation to the Unconscious*, *S.E.*, *8*.

—— (1905) *Three Essays on the Theory of Sexuality*, *S.E.*, *7*, 123.

—— (1907) 'Obsessive Actions and Religious Practices', *S.E.*, *9*, 116.

—— (1907) *Delusions and Dreams in Jensen's 'Gradiva'*, *S.E.*, *9*, 3.

—— (1908) ' "Civilized" Sexual Morality and Modern Nervous Illness', *S.E.*, *7*, 143.

239

—— (1910) 'A Special Type of Choice of Object made by Men (Contributions to the Psychology of Love, I)', *S.E.*, *11*, 165.
—— (1911) 'Psycho-Analytic Notes on an Autobiographical Account of a Case of Paranoia (Dementia Paranoides)', *S.E.*, *12*, 3.
—— (1912) 'On the Universal Tendency to Debasement in the Sphere of Love (Contributions to the Psychology of Love, II)', *S.E.*, *11*, 179.
—— (1912–13) *Totem and Taboo*, *S.E.*, *13*, 1.
—— (1913) 'The Claims of Psycho-Analysis to Scientific Interest', *S.E.*, *13*, 165.
—— (1914) 'Some Reflections on Schoolboy Psychology', *S.E.*, *13*, 241.
—— (1914) 'On Narcissism: an Introduction', *S.E.*, *14*, 69.
—— (1914) 'On the History of the Psycho-Analytic Movement', *S.E.*, *14*, 3.
—— (1914) 'The Moses of Michelangelo', *S.E.*, *13*, 211.
—— (1915) 'Instincts and their Vicissitudes', *S.E.*, *14*, 111.
—— (1915) 'Thoughts for the Times on War and Death', *S.E.*, *14*, 275.
—— (1916–17) *Introductory Lectures on Psycho-Analysis*, *S.E.*, *15–16*.
—— (1917) 'A Difficulty in the Path of Psycho-Analysis', *S.E.*, *17*, 137.
—— (1918) 'From the History of an Infantile Neurosis', *S.E.*, 17, 3.
—— (1920) *Beyond the Pleasure Principle*, *S.E.*, *18*, 7.
—— (1921) *Group Psychology and the Analysis of the Ego*, *S.E.*, *18*, 69.
—— (1922) 'Two Encyclopaedia Articles: Psycho-Analysis', *S.E.*, *18*, 235.
—— (1922) 'Two Encyclopaedia Articles: the Libido Theory', *S.E.*, *18*, 255.
—— (1923) *The Ego and the Id*, *S.E.*, *19*, 3.
—— (1924) 'The Dissolution of the Oedipus Complex', *S.E.*, *19*, 173.
—— (1925) *An Autobiographical Study*, *S.E.*, *20*, 3.
—— (1926) *The Question of Lay Analysis*. *S.E.*, *20*, 179.
—— (1926) *Inhibitions, Symptoms and Anxiety*, *S.E.*, *20*, 77.

—— (1927) 'Postscript to *The Question of Lay Analysis*', *S.E.*, *20*, 231.

—— (1927) *The Future of an Illusion*, *S.E.*, *21*, 3.

—— (1930) *Civilization and its Discontents*, *S.E.*, *21*, 59.

—— (1932) 'Why War? (A Letter to Einstein)', *S.E.*, *22*, 179.

—— (1932) 'Explanations, Applications and Orientations'. *New Introductory Lectures on Psycho-Analysis* (Lecture 34), *S.E.*, *22*, 136.

—— (1933) 'The Question of a *Weltanschauung*'. *New Introductory Lectures on Psycho-Analysis* (Lecture 35), *S.E.*, *22*, 158.

—— (1935) 'Postscript to *An Autobiographical Study*', *S.E.*, *20*, 71.

—— (1939) *Moses and Monotheism: Three Essays*, *S.E.*, *23*, 3.

—— (1954) *The Origins of Psychoanalysis: Letters to Fliess*, ed. E. Kris. New York: Basic Books.

Freud, S. & Abraham, K. (1907–26) *A Psychoanalytic Dialogue: the Letters of S. Freud and K. Abraham*, ed. H. C. Abraham and E. L. Freud. Hogarth Press, 1965.

Freud, S. & Zweig, A. (1927–39) *The Letters of Sigmund Freud and Arnold Zweig* ed. E. L. Freud. Hogarth Press, 1970.

Grunberger, B. (1956) 'Psychodynamic Theory of Masochism', in *Perversions*, ed. S. Lorand & M. Balint. New York: Random House.

—— (1971) *Narcissism: Psychoanalytic Essays*. New York: International Universities Press, 1979.

Jones, E. (1957) *The Life and Work of Sigmund Freud*, Vol. 3. New York: Basic Books.

Klein, M. (1929) 'The Importance of Symbol-Formation in the Development of the Ego', *International Journal of Psycho-Analysis*, *11* (1930), 24–39.

—— (1961) *Narrative of a Child Analysis*. Hogarth Press.

Laplanche, J. & Pontalis, J. B. (1973) *The Language of Psychoanalysis*. Hogarth Press.

Malinowski, B. (1929) *The Sexual Life of Savages*. Routledge.

Marchi, L. de (1973) *Wilhelm Reich: Biographie d'une Idée*. Paris: Fayard.

Marcuse, H. (1964) *One-Dimensional Man*. Routledge, 1968.

—— (1966) *Eros and Civilization*. Boston: Beacon Press.

—— (1968) Interview in *L'Express* (23 September), no. 898.

Marx, K. (1844) 'The Jewish Question' (a reply to Bruno Bauer) and 'The German Ideology', in *Marx and Engels*. Fontana, 1969.

Neill, A. S. (1913) *The Free Child*. London, 1953.

Nunberg, H. (1948–65) *The Practice and Theory of Psychoanalysis*. New York: Nervous and Mental Disease Monographs.

Ollendorf, I. (1969) *Wilhelm Reich*. Elek Books.

Orgone Energy Bulletin (1949–52) New York: Orgone Institute Press.

Palmier, J. M. (1969) *Wilhelm Reich*, 10/18. Paris: Plon.

Reich, W. (1919) 'Libidinal Conflicts and Delusions in Ibsen's *Peer Gynt*', in *Early Writings*. New York: Farrar, Straus & Giroux, 1975.

—— (1921) 'Drive and Libido Concepts from Forel to Jung', in *Early Writings*.

—— (1923) 'Concerning the Energy of the Drives', in *Early Writings*.

—— (1923) 'On Genitality', in *Early Writings*.

—— (1925) 'Further Remarks on the Therapeutic Significance of the Genital Libido', in *Early Writings*.

—— (1927) 'Discussion on Lay Analysis', *International Journal of Psycho-Analysis*, 8, 252–5; also in Reich (1952).

—— (1927) *The Function of the Orgasm*. Condor Books, 1983.

—— (1927–33) *Character Analysis* (3rd edn.). New York: Orgone Institute Press, 1949.

—— (1929) *Dialectical Materialism and Psychoanalysis*. (Printed with S. Bernfeld's 'Socialism and Psychoanalysis'.) Socialist Reproduction. (57 Jamestown Road, London NW1.)

—— (1930–36) *The Sexual Revolution*. New York: Farrar, Straus & Giroux, 1974.

—— (1931) *The Invasion of Compulsory Sex Morality*. New York: Farrar, Straus & Giroux, 1971.

—— (1932) 'The Masochistic Character', in *Character Analysis* (1949).

—— (1932) *The Sexual Struggle of Youth*. Socialist Reproduction, 1971.

—— (1933) *The Mass Psychology of Fascism*. New York: Simon & Schuster, 1970.

—— (1938) *Die Bione*. (Klinische und Experimentale Berichte, Nr. 6.) Berlin: Sexpol Verlag.

—— (1942) *The Discovery of the Orgone*, Vol. 1: *The Function of the Orgasm*. Condor Books, 1973.

—— (1948) *The Discovery of the Orgone*, Vol. 3: *The Cancer Biopathy*. New York: Orgone Institute Press.

—— (1949) *God, Ether and the Devil*. New York: Farrar, Straus & Giroux.

—— (1952) *Reich Speaks of Freud*. Condor Books, 1972.

—— (1952) *The Murder of Christ*. Condor Books, 1972.

—— (1952) *The Einstein Affair*. New York: Orgone Institute Press.

—— (1955) *The Cosmic Superimposition*. New York: Farrar, Straus & Giroux, 1975.

Rieff, P. (1966) *The Triumph of the Therapeutic*. Harmondsworth: Penguin Books, 1973.

Renan, E. (1881) 'Discours et Conférences', in *Oeuvres Complètes*, Vol. 1. Paris: Calmann-Lévy, 1947.

Robert, M. (1964) *The Psychoanalytic Revolution*. Allen & Unwin.

Rycroft, C. (1971) *Reich*. Fontana.

Séchéhaye, M. (1950) *Autobiography of a Schizophrenic Girl*. New York: Grune & Stratton.

Solzhenitsyn, A. (1972) 'Paix et Violence, Hypocrisie de l'Occident', *Contrepoint*, 12. (1 rue du Mail, Paris.)

Stéphane, A. (1969) *L'Univers contestationnaire*. Paris: Payot.

—— (1970) 'L'Amphithéâtre de Freud – Che Guevara', *Contrepoint*, 1.

—— (1970) 'Malaise dans la Civilisation: Freud et l'usage qu'on en fait', *Contrepoint*, 4.

—— (1971) 'L'Anti-Oedipe ou la Fin d'un Malentendu'. *Contrepoint*, 7–8.

243

—— (1971) 'Pour une définition psychanalytique de l'idéologie', *Contrepoint*, 12.
Tausk, V. (1919) 'On the Origin of the "Influencing Machine" in Schizophrenia', in *The Psychoanalytic Reader*, ed. R. Fliess. Hogarth Press, 1950.

INDEX

This edition of
Freud or Reich?
was finished in February 1986.

It was set in 11/13½ pt Baskerville
on a Linotron 202 phototypesetter
and printed by a Harris cold-set webb offset press
on Publishers' Antique Wove 80g/m² vol.19 paper.

The translation was commissioned by
Robert M. Young, edited by Claire Pajaczkowska,
designed by Carlos Sapochnik and produced
by Free Association Books.